I0642164

Mira Eldredge

Drops of Water From Many Fountains

Mira Eldredge

Drops of Water From Many Fountains

ISBN/EAN: 9783337143978

Printed in Europe, USA, Canada, Australia, Japan

Cover: Foto ©Andreas Hilbeck / pixelio.de

More available books at **www.hansebooks.com**

DROPS OF WATER

FROM

MANY FOUNTAINS.

BY

MIRA ELDREDGE.

"WHOSOEVER DRINKETH OF THE WATER THAT I SHALL GIVE HIM
SHALL NEVER THIRST."

NEW YORK:

FOSTER, & PALMER, JR., 14 BIBLE HOUSE.

1867.

Entered, according to Act of Congress, in the year 1866, by

FOSTER, & PALMER, JR.,

In the Clerk's Office of the District Court of the United States for
the Southern District of New York.

.

Stereotyped and Printed by
GEO. C. RAND & AVERY, Cornhill Press.

CONTENTS.

I.

INTRODUCTORY.

UR only apology for offering this little work to the public is the great want of the heart for spiritual suggestion and instruction. Much of our inner life is left sterile and barren, because no drops of living water fall upon its surface, vivifying and sanctifying its hidden springs.

Most of our literature exhausts itself upon the imagination, and fails to percolate down through the moral being, bringing it up to that high standard, where, united to Christ, we may "grow in grace" daily.

Many are thirsting for the higher life; but the well is deep, and they do not know how to draw from its mysterious depths.

We have aimed, in giving these desultory passages of experience, taken from letters received and written by the writer, to suggest the way of holy living. "By faith ye stand." We must be united to Christ by a living, energetic faith; and, to have that faith, we must have a corresponding energetic life, perfect obedience, perfect acquiescence to the Divine Will,—that love which "beareth all things, believeth all things, hopeth all things, endureth all things," "till we come, in the unity of the faith and of the knowledge of the Son of God, unto a perfect man, unto the measure of the stature of the fulness of Christ."

II.

FAITH.

Y life-path for a few days has been like terraced steps. No sooner had I ascended one steep of difficulty, than another, still higher, awaited my ascent. But to-day is one of victory. Like Moses, when he ascended Mount Sinai to receive the answer to his prayer, " Show me thy glory," so have I, of late, been ascending the mount; and to-day I stand upon the summit, by faith, alone with God. He lets his glory pass before me, and

7

gives me audience with the Holy Trinity. Oh,
how my heart has been gladdened and my
soul expanded at the near approach of the
Godhead,—three in one! The Holy Spirit has
revealed God to me a kind, tender Father;
Christ a present and all-sufficient Saviour;
and himself my Sanctifier, Comforter, and
Guide. Blessed faith! that reveals to us the
mysteries of godliness.

I am conscious that the daily discipline I am
receiving adds strength and force to my Christian character. But how slow am I to learn!
Were it not that God is so good and patient
in teaching me, I should be left to my own
ways, weak and unfruitful. Even now, with
all of God's love and condescension, I am
ever erring, and need the rod to goad me
on, lest I loiter by the way till death and
destruction overtake me.

Looking out these sunny days, so still and calm, the soul catches glimpses of peace. There is something very sweet in thinking of perfect tranquillity. How happy the soul that abides in quietness! It is easy so to live when we leave all with Jesus. The instantaneous turning all over to him gives no room for ruffled thoughts. Sweet is that habit of casting our burden on the Lord! Some one has said, "The ocean takes the hue of the sky toward which it looks; so the soul becomes like Christ by gazing upward." *I* become like Christ if I keep looking at him. Oh, what a great, incomprehensible thought! Yet faith grasps it.

"I am my beloved's: his desire is toward me." How sweet! how tender ! — the desire of Christ toward me — even me — as the bridegroom toward the bride. " Thou art fairer to me, my beloved, than all the trees of the wood." I find no true satisfaction in the things of earth. My chief joy is in Christ. If he were absent, earth would be a dark, barren waste.

Called on Mrs. N. this morning, and found her confined to her bed. She took my hand, saying, " What should we do without Jesus ? " All day my heart has echoed that, as, weak and weary from the morning exertion, the heart had been easily grieved with careless remarks that have fallen from depreciative lips.

How rich the Christian's legacy ! — " My peace I leave with you; my peace I give unto you." Praise God, it is mine! Perfect peace! For three weeks, nothing has moved me for a single moment. Such a depth of love too! I have enjoyed more during this time than I

once expected to enjoy in heaven. It is literally dwelling in God.

You ask if I am happy. Yes, H——; never
more so. I appreciate the full significance of
the lines, —

> "How happy is the Christian's lot!
> How free from every earthly thought!"

Müller's principle has been mine the past year.
My prayer is short, "Give me, this day, my
daily bread;" but it is always answered, and
my needs supplied. Oh this blessed life of
trust!—how safe with God! Oh this unmoved
experience! — what heaven-like repose, what
untold bliss! — a joy forever! I seldom have
sad hours now. They arise from a distrustful
state of mind, a dissatisfaction with the circumstances under which we are placed, a writhing
under needful discipline. I have learned not to

regard circumstances so much as He who controls them, and to remember that He who chooses our path for us is infinitely wiser than we.

Did it ever occur to you how many of the promises were introduced by, "They that trust in the Lord"? I am not surprised that they are not more frequently verified, because we do not *trust*, which is the condition.

Clouds in nature, but sunshine in the soul.

Christ does not regard our trials according to their character or degree alone, but according to their effect upon the heart. Blessed sympathizer! He sees as man cannot see. He alone can fully understand us. It is these little heartaches that are ever neglected by the world, but not by Jesus.

How firm a foundation, how safe a hiding-place, is my blessed Jesus! My crumb for days has been, "Fret not thyself because of evil-doers." "He never gives strength for coming ill until its advent."

My spirit is so calm this morning, and every morning! Oh, such a depth of peace, that even the whirlwinds of sorrow fail to produce a ripple upon its surface! This has been the general character of my experience since I left you: only occasionally there comes a wave of joy that so fills my soul with rapture, that the weak body cries out for pain; and I have to ask God to stay the tide of glory, and only fold me gently to his bosom, while he all his fulness shows.

I wish I could whisper a few living words to you. Do you not feel stronger for sympathy?

Oh, I can do so much when I am loved! Are
you not glad we have such a wealth of love
in the Saviour? Just now he whispers to us,
saying, "As the Father hath loved me, so
have I loved you : continue ye in my love."

It is one of autumn's gray, chilly days. My
heart is feeling a little autumnish, and yet not
quite in harmony with the day; but more like
one of those rich, mellow days in October,
when every thing is flooded with glory. The
spring buds of life's childhood have matured ;
the bright hopes of youth have blossomed and
flourished : but the summer-time of youth's
romance has faded, and left an autumn rich in
fruit, and crowned with a divine glory. I
thank God to-day that the lessons of life have
not been in vain. I feel their sacred, refin
ing influence upon my heart; and, while I
hold the hand of my Guide with a steady

faith, I am led into green pastures, and down by the peaceful waters of a holy rest.

The sanctified one seems to me like a vessel which God takes up to heaven, and fills with his love and power, and then returns to the church and the world to impart of the fulness of its salvation. It is by such that God has access to those so far away from him, that they do not hear the Spirit's whisperings. "The secret of the Lord is with them that fear him." "Blessed is the man to whom the Lord revealeth his secrets." Sweet privilege to be thus taken into the inner chambers of our Beloved! Blessed interchange of thought between the soul and the High and Holy One that inhabiteth eternity!

How humble we shall feel in heaven as we drink in the beauties and revelations of eter-

nity! We shall feel our utter nothingness as
we cannot imagine here.

Did you see the beautiful northern sky the
other evening? There was a path of purest
white completely spanning the heavens, like a
snowy rainbow. It was really sublime. How
we catch glimpses of the power and wonderful
skill of our God through his works! "His
greatness is unspeakable; his ways, past
finding out." And yet he loves us poor children.

These past weeks of suffering have been
indescribable as I have stood down by the
dark river; but my soul has been so sweetly
stayed in God! The darkness, even, was beautiful, like the twilight of a long summer's day,
— darkness that seemed born of light, shadows
ready to burst with glory; while the silvery

accents of the voice of Jesus were ever heard
above the dashing of the deep waters, saying,
" When thou passest through the waters, I will
be with thee." I had no unusual joy, but such
a strong faith, that all the powers of darkness
could not shake my trust in God. I knew
whom I believed. My will was wholly lost in
God's. Life or death I did not choose ; and
when I was bid to return, and take again
the burden of life, instead of receiving
my " crown of rejoicing," my willing heart
whispered, " Even so, Father ! Meekly will I
bear my cross of pain till fully prepared for
the many mansions."

What an inexhaustible resource we have in
the precious Bible ! Feeling burdened, I read,
" Cast your burden on the Lord : " but the
load seemed so heavy, I could not lift it up to
" cast " it upon him ; and, turning to the

margin, I found it, " Roll your burden upon God." It was *the* word to my weary soul. I could in passive trust let the burden fall, and feel Christ an all-sufficiency. Thank God, who supplieth all our needs.

I find each advanced step has its corresponding experience, and that of the last ascent has been so rich and glorious! The time has passed so pleasantly in sweet converse with God! O holy friendship! how indispensable to my momentary happiness! Is not this abiding in Christ, walking by faith, running with patience? Yes, Jesus assures me! Present, all-sufficient Redeemer! If he hides his face for a moment, my soul cries out for him, my beloved, my soul-satisfying portion.

The future seems dark to me; but, if I am doing rightly, God will sustain and bless.

> " These surface-troubles come and go
> Like rufflings of the sea."

Anxieties will come into the heart; but, notwithstanding these " surface-troubles," there is a deep undercurrent of continual trust. The Christian life is a mystery, — such a strange mingling of doubts and assurances, of fear and courage! but faith is the strong anchor-hold of the soul. We may be tossed about; but we cannot be wrecked.

My days are very like April days, blue sky and clouds. One moment the shower; the next repeating the words of inspiration, " I will trust, and not be afraid."

My soul prospers, leaning upon Jesus' bosom. Sweet resting-place for the weary !

> " As some rare perfume in a vase of clay
> Pervades it with a fragrance not its own ;
> So, when thou dwellest in a mortal soul,
> All heaven's own sweetness is around it thrown."

Exceeding great and precious promises has God given unto us: " Consider the ravens, and God feedeth them : how much more are ye better than the fowls! Not a sparrow falleth to the ground without your heavenly Father's notice."

The providences of God may seem to you dark and mysterious now; but let not your vague questionings rob you of the blessed consolation that God overrules all things, — even the smallest circumstances that shape our destiny. God has made certain general laws, such as would best be adapted to men as nations and individuals. He knew what would be from the beginning to the end, and made man a free moral agent, to be controlled by his law, or to repel it. Hence God's 'will reached all, and all things, either causing or permitting. He who watches the rise and fall of nations notes the sparrow's fall. He

who gives the planets their orbits orders the
steps of his children ; instructing them in the
way that they shall go, and guiding them with
his eye. He who gives to each leaf its form
and tint marks each falling tear, and hears the
sufferer's sigh. God is love. But you ask,
" Why so much sorrow and pain in earth ? "
Suffering is a heavenly discipline, a minis-
try of love. God would have the affections
of his creatures ; but they are constantly
making to themselves idols : hence the re-
moval. If our characters admit a large
development, God schools us according to
our temperament and need ; making usually
the path of duty to cross that of inclination.
The best often suffer the most. Why ? Do
not the choice minerals, the precious stones,
admit of the most burnishing, the most polishing, which brings out their brilliancy and
perfection ? So those that bring forth fruit

he purges, that they may bring forth more
fruit.   Yield your heart to God, your Father.
Bend the knee, asking wisdom and faith, and
light will gleam upon your path, which is
now shrouded in mist and darkness.

"Oh! is it hard to work for God?"

Leaning upon Christ, my staff and stay,
the shadow of a great rock in a weary land,
each Marah and Elim of the way brings us
nearer to Him, the home of the soul.

The day has been peculiarly adapted to a
dreamy state of mind.   Have been fitful and
fanciful.   Life seems like a long dream, un-
broken but by waking realities.   Now its
memories are bright and golden ; and again
they are shrouded in shadows so dark, that
faith alone can see the light behind the
veil.

Was very sad for a few moments ; and then
the grace which Jesus so sweetly rolled in
upon the soul completely submerged it all,
and I forgot the surroundings in the full enjoyment of Him whom my soul loveth.

Was very happy during the night ; but the
waters have been still and deep to-day. A
constant exercise of faith has subdued emotion.
Oh this steady, blessed reliance on God! "The
Lord is my shepherd : I shall not want."

" And I smiled to think God's goodness
shone round our incompleteness ; round our
restlessness, his rest." God fits us for our
individual work as he pleases.

Darkness enshrouds my earth-path ; but
there is light above. I am living by faith,
not by sight. Precious, precious Jesus ! I love

to fly to thee in hours of loneliness and sorrow. Thou knowest just what our little trials are to us; and in thy blessed heart of love thou dost hide us from the rude blast.

How often do we find that blessed promise verified in our experience, "In all thy ways acknowledge Him, and he shall direct thy paths"! Sometimes our ways are in the thick, dark forest; and we are often left to ourselves, that we may learn how weak and insufficient we are to keep and guide our steps. But, if we walk in the light of faith, our path shall be peaceful and serene; for God shall dwell in us, and God himself is light.

I have been having a surprise. "And he said unto them, When I sent you without purse or scrip or shoes, lacked ye any thing? and they answered, Nothing." I have lacked

shoes, and have had to borrow stockings and
rubbers, of late; but the Lord supplieth the
wants of the needy. My surprise included
a pair of boots, and the other day I had two
pairs of nice socks given me. Now I can
answer with the disciples, " Nothing."

O depths of iniquity, to need such discipline! O Infinite Love, to bear so long!
Though the furnace is heated very hot, yet
I pass through the fire, and am not burned;
neither is the smell of fire upon my garments.
" This is the victory that overcometh, even
our faith." Thank God, thank God! Though
the Red Sea of trial stretches out before me,
seemingly impassable, yet my faith takes hold
upon God. He who has led me thus far will
open a way for my feet; for the word of the
Lord standeth sure: " He delivereth them
out of all their troubles."

When reading the history of the Church, the fearful trials and sufferings of the saints of God, " of whom the world was not worthy," the question often arises, Why did God permit those wicked men to trample his people under their feet? (for nothing can happen to God's people without his permission.) And as I have looked at the matter carefully and prayerfully in the light of eternity, and in the light of God's word, I have come to the conclusion, that it is permitted for the best good of God's people, that, when the season of affliction is past, they may receive " a far more exceeding and eternal weight of glory ; " also that the cause they have espoused may be advanced, and God glorified. Truly the blood of the martyrs has been the seed of the Church. They have given a glorious demonstration to all men, — a demonstration which even confounds the infidel. That religion which enables them to endure so much, yea, even to rejoice in tribulation, must be divine.

> " Oh for a faith that will not shrink,
> Though pressed by every foe ! "

Nature is cloudy and sunless. We need sunshine in the heart when the natural sun stays away so long. Jesus whispers, " Thou art ever with me, and all that I have is thine."

How easy for God to take care of us when we will let him ; to make springs in the desert, and barren places fruitful !

Last sabbath was a very precious day to me. In the morning, a thought was presented by a brother, which was food for my soul all day : " The grace we possess is the measure of our faith." The Spirit whispered, " Then the measure of my faith must be the measure

of my need;" and, collecting the powers of
the soul, my faith was able to measure all the
fulness there is in Christ, and I was filled
with unutterable peace. Ever since, I have
been basking in the sunshine of God's presence. "His banner over me is love."

Shadows rested upon my heart; but they
are now flying fast before the rising Sun of
Righteousness. Earthly clouds often become
my telescope of heaven. "In our pilgrimage
here, we must have the bitter herbs with our
passover lamb."

How much unseen work these hearts perform! Have been tempted, sad, and grieved
all day; but at evening the shadows parted,
and I saw the promised light through the rift
of the cloud. "If afflicting mercy be so
sweet, what must be crowning mercy?"

From a pathway all shrouded in mist and
fear, I have stepped out into the broader and
more comforting way of a quiet trust and confidence in God. The long years of haunting
anxieties are gone, I trust, forever. Such a
change! Oh this precious trust! I verily
believe that this life of faith is far more desirable than a life of sight.

These words have been of great comfort:
" I know thy works, and where thou dwellest ;
even where Satan's seat is." Yes, " all, all, is
known to Thee ;" and yet are we permitted to
" go and tell Jesus " in our many and press-
ing needs.

Have had grandly glorious views of God,
as the one high over all. All his dealings
are in love and tenderness. " Sorrows are like
clouds, which are dark while we are passing

through them; but, when they are overpast,
they are like the garments of God, thrown off
in purple and gold."

I thank God for those days when every
thing seems to go wrong. It is in stemming
the current that we are conscious of growing
strength. It is in the struggle that nerve
and power are developed. Help me, O Lord!
to keep my face as a flint Zionward; that
I be not overcome of evil, but overcome evil
with good.

Felt sad on waking this morning; but
turned my tearful eyes as naturally to Jesus
as the flower turns its dewy petals to the
morning beams.

Am still under the cloud. Have great
mental and physical lassitude. I cannot

think God withholds his smiles because we do not try as hard to please him as at other times; for we do really make more effort in these seasons of darkness. We pray more, the heart yearns more intensely for our seemingly absent Lord; while, when we are permitted to behold his smiles, our only effort is to *enjoy* him.

I love to think of God in Christ, because he seems so merciful, tender, and willing — oh, so willing! — to forgive, and yet so far off. But Jesus is nigh. What do those do who believe not in Christ's divinity? From what source do they draw comfort? Jesus is the only name that soothes our sorrows, and quiets disturbed and restless thoughts. Christ's love is like the wing of God spread over us in our fear and trembling of the great I Am.

Have felt it such a privilege to continue
with Christ in suffering! "A place by Me."
How happy the soul that is kept close to God!
— even like the little child, who knows no
fear in its repose upon the maternal bosom.

Look up! the reflection of the heavenly
light of trust will make earth's dark scenes
even glorious.

Sometimes God seems to leave us for a season, as he did Jesus in the wilderness ; but if
we trust him with childlike confidence, if we
cling to him with fidelity, with what feelings
of pleasure and satisfaction he must regard
us, even while we think he frowns upon us !
"Sorrow at our inability to pray is communion with God."

Our varied experience reveals to us the different attributes in the character of Christ, so that sometimes we catch glimpses of all the fulness that dwells in him. Blessed Jesus! reach down thy hand, and lead me safe through earth's night.

Have felt very sick for a few days; but Christ has been peculiarly precious and near to pity and comfort. "He stayeth his rough wind in the day of the east wind," always adapting our strength to the cross. Strength in my weakness! Blessed One! how instinctively my heart turns away from every thing of earth to thee! None but Jesus; none but Jesus.

God's love is unchanging, ever the same. Though we are constantly vacillating, "Thou art, from everlasting to everlasting, God; the same, yesterday, to-day, and forever." In our wanderings, thou dost not forget us, but pity-ingly dost love us still.

I had expected such a result, and had been nerving myself for it; so that, when the blow came, I had only to stretch out arms of faith, and, clinging to Christ, I was safe. How could I sink with such a prop as the eternal God! Such perfect resignation as was given me! Anywhere, any thing : I was satisfied since I had Jesus. Infinite strength to bear a finite trial.

Let me tell you a little of an hour I spent with God a few evenings since. It was an experience new, and superior to any thing I had before realized. It was a calm, steady concentration of the powers of the soul upon God, to that extent, that it seemed like a conversation of friend with friend. My spirit-vision became so charmed with the view of God, that when I turned my eyes again to the earth, after gazing upward for an hour, I felt that I could fully appreciate Paul's experience as expressed in 2 Cor. xii. God revealed to me something of his design in dealing with me as he had in the past, and something of his purposes respecting the future. He so took me into his confidence, that I had new and very enlarged ideas of faith and its results. "Blessed is the man to whom the Lord revealeth his secrets."

When first this realization opened to my view, cutting off the hope of present recovery, I felt the cross greatly increase in weight; it pressed me sore ; and, in my struggle of soul, I cried out, "All Thy waves and Thy billows are gone over me!" But in a calm, steady exercise of faith, I clung to Christ so closely,

that the next outburst of my heart was, "Even
so, Father; for so it seemeth good in thy sight."
I need to be made holier, and I shall not have
one pain more than my Father sees is needful
for me. I desire not my crown till my measure of suffering is full.

I often sigh for the fellowship of kindred
spirits, but never have the oppressive sadness
of other days. I praise God for such a deliv-
erance, and for the experience so new and
sweet. Such an undisturbed peace! I seldom
think I have trials now; and, when circumstances are not agreeable to my feelings, I
consider them the " need be's" of life. " Your
heavenly Father knoweth that ye have need
of these things."

I have for weeks past dwelt beneath the
shadow of Calvary, close to the cross. How

holy is the atmosphere here ! I am constantly beholding new beauties in Christ. Oh, may my eyes never turn away from beholding him, the Lamb of God, the blessed Lamb, that cleanseth the heart from guilt !

There are none here who seem fully to understand me ; but I turn my eyes upward, and I see One with loving arms outstretched. By faith I throw myself into his embrace. I lean my head against his great " mother-heart," and feel that he loves me, owns me for his child, and fully understands and appreciates my feelings. This is my Saviour, precious and loving, — ever near to make me happy, and throw gleams of sunshine upon my solitude.

I cannot doubt God's goodness, though what seems to me blessings are withheld. I fear not to press my way on, though the way before me is dark, because I am clinging to Jesus, and he has promised to be with me to the end. I need not be fearful of following while the divine arm is underneath me. "The foundation of God standeth sure." It is well with me, and will be. I cannot doubt God.

> " Oft, when I seem to tread alone
>> Some barren waste with thorns o'ergrown,
>> Thy voice of love in tenderest tone
>>> Whispers, ' Still cling to me.'
>> Though faith and hope awhile be tried,
>> I ask not, need not, aught beside :
>> How safe, how calm, how satisfied,
>>> The soul that clings to thee ! "

I am hid under the " feathers " of the Almighty (Ps. xci.). The rude blasts of earth cannot chill me. Safe, secure shelter.

A deep, rich joy fills my soul. I feel that

I have a "present heaven." But if this be heaven, with so much sorrow and pain, " what must it be to be there ?" How I wish all could know of this strong reliance upon God, while on their pilgrimage, — this perfect trust in him, this sweet repose of faith !

These are precious lessons that we learn in the furnace. How plainly we can see that all things *do* work together for good ! As earthly ties lessen, the heart rests more securely upon God and heaven. I realize as never before what it is to be in the world, and yet not of it. I desire to live only for the good of others. It is so pleasant to be a worker in the vineyard ! Sweet toil for Jesus ; and, by and by, sweet and perfect rest with Jesus.

When my sins and imperfections appear in full array, I dare not dwell upon them, but

turn away to the wounded Saviour; and,
while I gaze at the flowing tide, I forget
all, only that Jesus saves me, that his blood
cleanses from all sin. Oh blessed atonement!
precious, precious blood! one drop can can-
cel our entire guilt. Glory, glory to Jesus!
Catch the strains as you read, and whisper it
too; for it makes the heart, way down deep,
so glad! Hark! I hear spirit-voices in the
distance, singing, "Glory, honor, power, belong
to the Lamb who was slain for us!" I sometimes wish we had a heavenly vocabulary, it is
so hard to define this spiritual life in this dull
language.

God does not give us an abundance of grace,
and fill our earthen vessels, simply for our
enjoyment alone; but there are corresponding trials, and constant tests to our
faith. Amid the series through which I have

passed, my heart has been stayed upon God, and I felt that it was through the Spirit alone that I conquered. How grateful I am for trial! I often look up with tearful eyes, and thank God for this and that one; for I find that each is a means in divine use to purify the heart.

On account of neuralgia in the head, I have not been able to enjoy as much of God's sensible presence for a few days. It has seemed as if he had gone a long journey. Sweet Jesus! I pine for thy smiles; and faith brings to the spirit's hearing the sweet words, "Thou art ever with me, and all that I have is thine." How I love the experience of faith! It is so quiet and calm! Sick or well, we can trust. Ah! whither should I flee, were not God my refuge?

I am joyfully counting " all but loss for the

excellency of the knowledge of Christ Jesus my Lord." If the Captain of our salvation became perfect through suffering, I would walk in the same thorny but hallowed steps of my Lord.

What a mighty power is love! I am trying to get hold of God's power. I think I have not expected the mightiest results from my feeble efforts. The prophet says, "The Lord God is my strength." Oh that I may realize this, and become mighty to the pulling-down of the strongholds of the enemy!

So happy! My heart is very full of joy, because God dwells therein, and is the joy thereof. Feel like whispering his praise continually.

As I kneeled down, feeling just a little sad,

as the realization pressed itself upon my heart of the instability of earthly things, the Spirit suggested, "Thou art, from everlasting to everlasting, God,—the same, yesterday, to-day, and forever." "Yes," my heart exclaimed, "always God!" Not like earthly joy, bright to-day, and clouded to-morrow, but always God! What a comforting thought! a source of joy, a staff and a stay amid earth's mutability. "Behold, He that keepeth Israel shall neither slumber nor sleep." God does not sicken, nor his heart of love grow cold. In all conditions, under all circumstances, he is always God; "and beside him there is none else."

"By whose stripes we are healed." We, wounded and bleeding with iniquity, healed through Christ's sufferings and death; made whole in the hour in which we believe in the great sacrifice for sin! Blessed Jesus! thy love, thy condescension, thy life of self-sacrifice, thy ignominious death, draws us to thee. We come, thou bleeding Lamb! Thine we are.

As I thought, last evening, how few there were that understood me, how few there were familiar with my inner life, I looked fully away to Jesus; and he folded me tenderly to his warm, palpitating heart of love, and whispered, "Lo, I am with you alway." As I thought of him an ever-constant friend, and seeming to appreciate, too, our effort at constancy and fidelity, in that he acknowledged, " Ye are they who have continued with me," the tears of joy flowed down my cheeks, while I sat long at the cross, gazing up at my Beloved, and satisfying my ravished soul with the glory of his grace. Thus am I daily dying to self;

thus is my life in Christ growing deeper and broader day by day.

Awoke many times in the night, and whispered, "Glory to Jesus!" My heart was overflowing with love. The very atmosphere seemed heavenly, and the whole place was full of his glory. Glory, glory, to Jesus!

This word has been so precious to my heart all day,—"saved!" Yes, saved through the blood of the Lamb,—washed and made clean, whiter than the snow. Thank God, thank God! Our poor lives are all covered up with Christ.

My soul is full of glory. Jesus all the day long is my joy. A joy forever is my Beloved. My meditation of him is sweet. Fresh every morning and new every evening are his mercies to my soul.

I am leaning upon the Omnipotent Arm.
All will be well. God knows best. I am
wonderfully supported day by day, as I dwell
upon the fearful trial that awaits me. Was
greatly comforted by the twelfth of Isaiah:
"I will trust, and not be afraid." — "God is
too wise to err." I can fully rely upon Him
"who sticketh closer than a brother." Was
unable to go out to church to-day; but in my
suffering I cling to Jesus, and whisper, —

> "As God will;
> And in his mighty hand hold still."

These continued kindnesses burden my
heart more than if everybody's hand were
against me. Oh, how sweetly will it fall upon
the ears of some of God's children, "Inas-
much as ye have done it unto the least of
these my brethren, ye have done it unto me"!
With that consideration, that it is done for

Christ's sake, I can bear to receive; for he can reward so abundantly!

I do not have doubts now. They are of no use: they make me so restless and unhappy! If one fastens itself on me, I begin all anew, and say, "If I never have been a Christian, I will be one from this moment." My soul all the week has been crying out so strongly for Christ, feeling that I possess so little of his real life and spirit! Even in my half-wakeful hours, the heart seems reaching out for God; and I have such an increasing desire to have an eye single to his glory!

I have stepped over the deep, dark chasm of unrest, fear, and doubt, and have passed into the green pastures, and down beside the still waters of simple faith in God. Things that once would have cast aside my confidence now increase it; and I move steadily, quietly, on towards home. Shadows of doubt come often over me; but, through Christ, I am able to come off conqueror. For me to live is Christ. His work is my work. I am not anxious for the future. I know, if I commit my way unto the Lord, he will bring it to pass.

> " My soul feeds on thy word,
> And strength receives from thee.
> I weary not of thee, my Lord:
> Oh! weary not of me."

I am realizing very fully the obligation that rests upon us to employ all the power which a full baptism of the Holy Ghost secures to us. Holiness is power. May our faith measure our need, and claim all that it is our privilege to have!

My heart is glad in the Lord all the time.

He keeps me. Thanks be to him! Thoughts of, " We are unto God a sweet savor of Christ," have been very sweet and cheering.

While suffering to-day, I read Paul's experience, " I glory in my infirmity." It found a response in my own heart; and I felt that I could glory in my pain, which is my infirmity, lest I should be exalted above measure.

The greatest folly of my life has been in not taking hold of Christ by faith. But I can now say, " Lord, I believe ;" and it brings repose and comfort. My religion does not afford me joy: it is simply quietness and trust. I do not think I shall ever know jubilant happiness ; but I am satisfied with the quiet repose of faith. The grand principle of religion is obedience, not emotion ; but

4

the best of my life passed in error, and I have not realized that comfort which God grants to those who readily and cheerfully obey. How many golden opportunities are gone forever! And yet may not each experience of life be a benefit, like the parts which go to make up the whole?

Am drinking from the Fountain-head, and my very soul is satisfied with fulness of joy. Fulness of joy in a " hundred-fold," with our poor human capacities; and " in Thy presence is fulness of joy " forever and forever.

> " No more fatigue, no more distress ;
> Nor sin nor pain shall reach the place ;
> No sighs shall mingle with the songs
> That warble from immortal tongues."

God is so very good! Am walking in the path of duty safely. All Christ's. Hid with Christ in God. Glory to Jesus!

Each little trial of the day is sweet. I thank God for all. How they drive me to the immutable source of joy and peace! I rejoice in the power of religion, — in the love of Jesus. I can bear to be excluded from the love of others; but his love I crave. How could I live without it?

This has been a blessed week. God has filled my heart with himself, and given me the sweet assurance that I was in the path of duty. I have not for a moment been led to doubt that I was acting contrary to God's will. Christ has been ever present, making the heart rejoice. Sweet Jesus,

"Thou art my soul's bright morning-star,
And thou my rising sun."

How many important lessons we learn in the "school of affliction"! Shut in from

the world, we have so many quiet opportunities of studying the heart, and correcting
the habits formed, and mistakes made, in the
hurry of active life! It is true, life is changed,
and to human vision seems sometimes

" All dark and barren as a rainy sea : "

but the light of hope and faith shines all the
more brightly for the surrounding darkness;
and, guided by its silvery gleams, I will press
on till the noonday light of the home of God
bursts upon my immortal view.

It seems as though I had grown to Christ;
and the giving-up of my hope is like severing
the branch from the vine. No, I cannot lay
it aside. The very thought shows me how
precious he has become to my heart, and how
necessary to my life.

Am trusting, — simply trusting. *All* things

are working for my good, not a *part* merely.
As I think of the past, there is no trial I would
have left out of my experience. Trials bring
my poor, haggard heart nearer heaven. Thank
God for all, every drop of my life-cup !

Another are broken from the home-
circle; another voice hushed; another seat
vacant. How unlike dark infidelity is our
blessed faith ! While the infidel mourns as
one without hope, we can rejoice that another
gem is added to the Saviour's coronet, — that
the voice hushed on earth is joining the
mighty chorus of " Worthy the Lamb that
was slain for us ! " Do you not think that
Jesus is happy to welcome back one after
another of his little ones as they come up
from their pilgrim-journey ? Heaven would be
incomplete to him without us : for he has said,
" They are mine ; my Father gave them me."

Ah, yes! He takes one after another to behold his glory, to partake of his joy, to enter into his rest.

Let me give you one sweet promise, — yours by virtue of the present affliction : "I have torn, and I will heal" (Hos. vi. 1). Let your faith now appropriate it to your present need. It will soothe and comfort your aching heart. O precious word! Gilead's balm ; the oil of joy for mourning.

For a week past, I have dwelt upon the Word with great comfort; have revelled in the green pastures of God's truth. How I want to have our blessed religion a greater reality, and Jesus an ever-present Saviour! What good are all these forms and ordinances, save as a means to bring us nigh unto our Beloved ? Miss Newton, in speaking of a sacramental occasion, says, "I have been catching glimpses of Jesus through the lattice-work of the ordinances."

I am trying to walk "circumspectly, redeeming the time." I have full faith in the blood of the Lamb. I am clinging to the Holy One, and carry my burdens to the cross, and leave them there.

> "And thou, O Lord! by whom are seen
> Thy creatures as they be,
> Forgive me, if too close I lean
> My human heart on thee."

The experience of the past week has been promiscuous indeed. Trial after trial has rolled in upon the soul like the waves of the ocean ; but steadily has the anchor of faith held me, sheltered in the haven of Christ, where the storms of life cannot reach to disturb the deep calm of the trusting heart.

"Forever here my rest shall be,
Close to thy bleeding side ;
This all my hope and all my plea, —
For me the Saviour died."

I so pitied poor Job as I read, " There is
no daysman between us, that might lay his
hand upon us both " (Job ix. 33). Christ is
so like a shield when we feel afraid of God
in his absolute holiness ! Sometimes I tremble
to draw near to God ; but Christ is so like a
friend, I dare approach him, rest in him, and
trust my all to him. Christ is my all; and
for me to live is Christ, and to die is gain.

Saved, fully saved, through the precious
blood of Christ ! Grace sufficient for each day.
Oh, how good is the Lord our God ! I do not
love him half enough. My heart seems all too
small. " Thy right hand hath holden me up,
and thy gentleness hath made me great."

Have been drawn very near to Christ to-day.
The commemoration of his death, the remem-
brance of his love, have melted my heart to
tenderness, and brought me very low at the
cross; and as I have there gazed up at my
dying Lord, the bleeding Lamb for sinners
slain, I have had new and vast conceptions of
the divine character, the very essence of which
is love, — divine, unchanging love.

I have very little time for meditation or
communion with God while school-duties
press me so hard. How sweet it will be when
in heaven we have nothing to detract from a
constant and steady intercourse with God, our
Father! Oh happy thought! oh wondrous
conception! — to study God throughout eternity, and to become more and more God-like
as the eternal ages roll! Press on, my weary
soul: the "little while" wanes fast.

A deep-abiding peace pervades my heart, and arms of love encompass me, — such arms as would all mankind embrace. Christ is my rock and my salvation, my covert from the storm, my Redeemer from all sin. Precious Christ! I know I love him with all my heart; and I know that he loves me, because he follows me with chastisement: "As many as I love, I rebuke and chasten." Precious Christ! precious when the shadows deepen and the storm gathers.

Sometimes we are led to question why God imposes such heavy burdens. He has promised, "My grace shall be sufficient:" then we are to infer, that, the greater the burden, the more abundant the grace. Surely the afflicted one is privileged; for, by virtue of the promises made to such, we can claim largely of divine strength and power. Can we not better glorify God in affliction in the use of the abundance of grace given, while we bear up under the load so trustingly, submissively, and cheerfully, showing to those about us the sustaining grace of God, and leading them to acknowledge, " We have not seen such great faith, no, not in Israel " ? There is a vast difference between submitting to God's will because there is no alternative, and loving it so that we would prefer what is sent to any thing else. .We can have the former without cheerfulness or comfort ; but the latter makes us so very happy ! How slow we are in learning to *love* our Father's will ! How kind and patient our God in the continuance of life's discipline ! He bears so long ! Yet would we pray, " Leave us not, neither forsake us."

Let the poor heart throw its burden into the bosom of Jesus. It is easy journeying then.

"Child, take my hand;
Cling close to me: I'll lead thee through the land.
Trust my all-seeing care, so shalt thou stand
'Midst glory bright above."

Afflicted one of earth, honored of God, strike your harp of praise; for great is the goodness of the Lord unto the children of men. You are surely one of God's peculiar ones, — one that he regards with special care; a precious stone that he is polishing and refining for the Saviour's coronet; cut off from earthly good, but rich in faith and the things of the kingdom.

"The eager hearts, the souls of fire,
    Who pant to work for God and man,
Who view with eyes of keen desire
    The upland way of toil and pain, —
Almost with scorn they think of rest,
Of holy calm, of tranquil breast;
But God, through ways they have not known,
    Will lead his own."

It will be so sweet to get home! But, oh, my life has been so imperfect! If I am saved, it will be all of Christ, — Christ's love for me. He will not live in glory, and leave us behind. No: he said he would come again, and take us to himself, — to *himself.* Sweet home of my soul, how near!

The blow came not heavily; but so gently did it fall upon the spirit, that it had time to rally, and stretch out its arms of faith, encircling the neck of Christ so closely, that I felt deeply and emphatically the power of an endless life bearing me up. I did not weep, — did not even feel sad. I thought not of foiled plans or crushed hopes. I had such a vivid conception of the depth of infinite love, that all else was swallowed up. Thank God for victory through Christ! Thank God for a power that enables us to rejoice in tribulation!

Catch the strain, ye heavenly hosts, and thank God for salvation for ever and ever.

Jesus is the great luminary of my soul amid earth's shadows.

> " What though a short eclipse his beauties shroud,
>   And bar the influence of his rays :
> 'Tis but a morning vapor or a summer cloud.
>   He is my sun, though he refuse to shine :
> Though for a moment he depart,
> I dwell forever on his heart,
>   Forever he on mine."

As darkness gathers about my way, the Comforter comes with words of cheer : —

> " My arms shall be around thee day by day ;
> My smile shall cheer thee on thy heavenly way."

With everlasting arms to encircle me, and the smile of the Holy One, all will be well.

I am bolstered up in bed this morning, with window wide open, drinking from God's deep, broad ocean of pure air. My heart feels large enough to take in a world; and nothing would so permeate it with intense joy as to be able to rise up and go forth, a laborer in the Master's vineyard. My cup is full as a sufferer; and it will surely run over with joy when I am permitted again to join the ranks of those going about to do good. Thank God, the long, dark night of pain is fading away, and the morning comes slowly.

Oh, my life, my life! What is it? What has it been? What may it be? Sometimes I dare not think; and again in my closet, with clasped hands and silent lips, the whole soul goes out in a "Thy will be done." My entire being is ever reaching on and on for something! Oh this indefinite something! And yet its base is in my own life, deeply and firmly laid; and the structure can only rise by my adding to it, daily, duties done well. Faith and hope lighten the darkness of seeming impossibilities; and, if not here the hungry soul be fed, "we shall be satisfied when we awake in His likeness."

Felt a little lonely to-day, as sympathy is the great want here ; but found it sweet to breathe my feelings to my heavenly Father. He whispered, "I love, I understand: child, lean on me." Was comforted on reading "Christ's kisses for thy watery cheeks, O tried believer!"

Rev. Mr. C——n has been in, passing an hour with me. My heart burns within me from the little talk we had of Jesus by the way. That soul-cheering prayer of faith reached the divine ear, and sweetly descends upon my heart the influence of heaven. Thank God for Christian sympathy!

Resting in God. How firm a basis for the trembling heart, that finds no resting-place in earth! The atmosphere within seems cold. The heart keeps hungering; but Christ keeps loving: so it is well, — it is well.

How slight is my suffering, compared to what Jesus suffered for me! Precious Jesus! Fulness of joy! Well of salvation! Oh for a faith to plunge into the ocean-fulness of his love, and to drink of the fountain of joy!

Am earnestly praying that my eyes may be turned away from vanity, and that I may " behold beauty in God's law." My readings of the Word are attended with more comfort of late. " Shall abide under the shadow of

the Almighty." What safety ! — never in danger there. " As the bridegroom rejoiceth over
the bride, so shall thy God rejoice over thee."
Imagine God rejoicing over us sinful, fallen
ones with the joy of a bridegroom over his
new-found treasure ; even seeming to make
us needful to his joy ! Again : he says he will
send forth the spirit of his Son into our hearts,
crying, " Abba, Father." What tender terms,
" Husband," " Father " ! Do they not encourage our confidence, and strengthen our trust ?
Jesus, too, is such a ready " elder Brother "
to be " touched with the feelings of our infir-
mities." Sometimes, when in suffering, I try
to pray, I am so comforted in thinking Jesus
prays for me. Yes, he has entered into the
holy of holies, and liveth to make intercession
for us.

As the glad music died away in the distance,

so faded the light of joy from out my heart.
Such are our earthly joys, ephemeral and
fleeting; "but in Me ye shall have peace."
Oh, how we cling to the Rock when every
thing is dashed upon the breakers of life!

> "God, through ways we have not known,
> Will lead his own."

Thick clouds darken the natural horizon ; but
the veil that hides the inner glory of heaven's
sanctuary seems very thin. While shut into
my closet alone with God, streams of heavenly
glory burst into my soul ; and the presence of
God filled all the place where I was kneeling.
To know more of Christ, and to exhibit his
loving, humble spirit in all my life, is my
ruling desire.

My heart is so strong in God ! The yoke of
Christ is easy, and his burden light. I rejoice
that I am counted worthy to be called a "fool

for Christ's sake ; " for God says, " Fear not.
Since thou wast precious in my sight, thou
hast been honorable, and I have loved thee."

"In darkest shades, if thou appear,
My dawning is begun :
Thou art my soul's bright morning-star,
And thou my rising sun."

Way down deep in the heart, I enjoy the
blessed realization that God doeth all things
well. Tenderly he watches each step of the
way his weary, burdened children tread. He
brings them by the way that leads most direct
to heaven. But it is only by faith that we are
able to appreciate this direct highway of the
soul. Hence, Lord, increase our faith, and
give us the elastic step of those who " run,
and are not weary."

When the heart is aching, and I sink under

life's heavy burden, I stay up the soul with repeating, "When thou passest through the waters, I will be with thee; and through the rivers, they shall not overflow thee."

> "All tearfully, all fearfully,
>   Alone and sorrowing,
> My dim eye lifted to the sky,
>   To thy dear cross I cling,
> O Christ! to thy dear cross I cling."

My quiet room seems the dwelling-place of God! I have but to look up, and I meet his smiles. My faith grows strong. I am confident my path will open by God's direction, and as is best adapted to me. God knows how purely alive our sensitive hearts are to suffering; and all that is possible to our happiness, social or spiritual, he gives.

> "He sendeth sun; He sendeth shower:
>   Alike they're needful to the flower."

"No good thing will He withhold from them that walk uprightly."

My heart is filled with a holy joy this morning. I find it pleasant to stay and suffer upon earth, when the spirit is so near heaven. Thank God that I have at last learned the lesson of perfect trust! I simply take God at his word, and he makes me happy anywhere and everywhere. I am more conscious of his companionship than of those around me. In the world, and yet not of it.

I have no one but Jesus. My poor, weary soul clings to him. He is my all. I call him mine.

"If a man love me, he will keep my words; and my Father will love him; and we will come unto him, and make our abode with

him." How plain the test of our love to God,
—keeping his words! How great the divine
condescension, " We will make our abode with
him"! Sweet is it to live where we can constantly feel the presence of God, and appre-
preciate the divine companionship. How
easy to grieve the Holy Spirit, and become
separated from Christ! God help that we may
walk with sacred awe, as did Moses before the
burning bush!

My heart is so very peaceful! I seem not to
feel the jar of earth's tumult. Nothing moves
me. All the circumstances of life are tem-
pered by the kind and gentle Shepherd.

Sweet and sure are the promises, full of
strength and comfort. The needed strength
comes moment by moment. I felt in school,
to-day, so fully swallowed up in God, that I

seemed not to be acting of myself, but controlled fully by some divine agency.

The discipline of the past has seemed to bring
me by the very shortest possible way to heaven.
Thank God! Sometimes, when faith is in
lively exercise, he seems to take us "across
lots," and not leave us to wander forty years
in the wilderness through unbelief.

> "Thine arm our souls can guard
> Safe through each passing hour."

Thank God! thank God! Sweet is it to run
in the way of Thy commandments.

Participated in a fine entertainment given
to our class last evening; but, during the
whole evening, I did not hear the name of Jesus mentioned once. My heart felt strange
and sad; and, when proper, I took my place by
the window, and, gazing out into the night,

communed with Him whom my soul loveth.
Precious was the tide of love that flowed into
my soul, and sweet the overshadowings of
His presence. Had felt a great want in the
conversations of the evening; but, when conversing with God alone, my soul was satisfied.
How sweet the sympathy of the Divine! strong
and abiding.

Tempted and tried! Have been constantly
struggling to call the promises all mine. Amid
the din of the conflict, I could hear the Saviour
say, " Your Father knoweth that ye have need
of all these things." While singing, " Jesus,
lover of my soul," I hid me under the shadow
of those outspread wings, and by faith was
made secure from the power of the Enemy.

I dare not look at the long panorama of life
as it stretches out before me; but I do dare to

grasp Christ's hand, and to " lay hold " of the Infinite One, whom I find as a strong tower. I cannot see into the dark future ; but I can trust One who knows the end from the beginning, and who knoweth them that are his.

These continued sunless days seem dreary. I quite pine for the sunshine.

> " No night shall be in heaven ; no gathering gloom
> Shall o'er that glorious landscape ever come."

He who has the sunlight of God's presence has continual day, — even heaven here. Have enjoyed dwelling upon " Blessed is the man that endureth temptation ; for, when he is tried, he shall receive a crown of life that fadeth not away." Endurance now ; but palms of glory and crowns of victory just upon the other side.

" Thou art ever with me, and all that I have is thine." How rich the child of God, though poor in this world's goods! Access to all of heaven! O ye hungry, barren souls! could ye but catch one glimpse of the fulness in Christ, ye would believe. "Lord, help our unbelief."

"Lead Thou me on;
Keep Thou my feet. I do not ask to see
The distant scene: one step enough for **me.**
Lead Thou me on."

"As the Father hath loved me, so have I loved you." What! the love that God bore to his dear Son the measure of Christ's love to us fallen ones? Wondrous thought! Love deep and incomprehensible! And yet faith grasps it; and I sink into the great deep, lost in wonder and praise. Thank God for such a salvation!

Such earnest desires as I have for more of

God, — the living God! These forms and ceremonies alone do not satisfy. I want an indwelling divinity, the door of the senses shut to the outward world, and a constant consciousness of God with me. Was interested while reading, "As clay in the hands of the potter." Will He not fashion us, so as to bring to Himself the most glory? "We are His workmanship, created unto righteousness."

"Behold me!" Have tried to keep my eye fixed so steadily upon Jesus, that, beholding him, I may be changed into the same image, from glory to glory.

Have been much alone, but have enjoyed the satisfying portion of God's companionship in an unusual degree. Have felt the force of Beecher's words: "God is multitudinous above all the nations of the earth."

Hanging to Christ! Sweet Christ! What
is he not to me? My pains are increasing;
but each is a Father's gift, — a marked blessing, yielding the peaceable fruits of righteousness.

I am permitted, while passing under the
cloud, to realize that I am but treading in the
footsteps of Jesus. How much the thought
softens the roughness of the way, and lightens
the darkness! Rough now; but the end thereof
is peace and everlasting joy in the presence of
our God.

How tenderly anxious the Saviour is for his
little ones! Have been much interested in the
incident of his walking to them upon the water.
How often he comes walking on the billows
of life to us, and saying, " Be not afraid: it
is I "!

"It is well, it is well, it is well!
 Though sorrow cloud our way,
'Twill make the joy more dear
 That ushers in the day."

I have very little variety of experience now. The will seems to be so wholly lost in the Father's, that I love every thing he sends. There is a divine calm in the heart, so that nothing seems to move me. I do not have any joy; not the definite peace that I have sometimes: but it is a passive, trusting state of soul, which gives me quiet and rest. I feel my vileness very sensibly, and every moment the need of the Saviour's blood. Every thought and act seem united with self; but I struggle hard to overcome, and God gives me quiet victories.

" Take my poor heart, and let it be
 Forever closed to all but Thee ;
 Seal Thou my breast, and let me wear
 The pledge of love forever there."

My heart says it, feels it, and revels in its beauty. I have given my heart all away to my Beloved. He is mine, and I am his, in an everlasting covenant.

We know " all things work together for good to them that love God ; " but it needs a strong faith always to enable us to say, " *We know*." Sometimes we look forward, and a Red Sea of trial stretches out before us : the way looks dark ; and reason says, " Why was this permitted ? " But, thanks be to our dear heavenly Father, his Spirit teaches us to say, " It is all right." How marvellous is the change wrought in us poor sinners ! Once blind, now we see. How shall we ever praise God enough ? Not here, not here ; but by and by we will praise him without weariness for ever and ever.

I feel that the soul is really and honestly struggling into light. It is daybreak with me now. How much there is to contend with! I rarely dream; yet, for two nights past, Satan has been so busy with my tired brain, that he has filled my sleeping hours with just those scenes that trouble me most when awake. I am praying to be so wholly the Lord's, that, even in sleep, I shall be abiding in him.

The other day I was trying to be good under adverse circumstances, when suddenly I showed ill-temper. Once it would have destroyed all peace, and I should have fallen into darkness and doubt: but, in a moment, I thought it was not intended,— it was a mistake, springing spontaneously from the force of habit; and I looked up, and cried, "Forgive me, Father, for Jesus' sake." At once I felt the blood of sprink-

ling applied. Will not God forgive *at once?*
Does he want tears and pleadings long?
I was sorry, — so sorry, that I have not
failed in that point since. "In His love
and in His pity he redeemed them." Love
and pity, — love and pity: I so love these
precious words!

Oh that poor, weary, tempest-tossed souls
could take all of Christ to bear their heavy
burdens with! "If ye abide in me, and my
words abide in you, ye shall ask what ye will,
and it shall be done unto you." All of Christ!
He, in the hour of temptation, had his divinity
to throw himself back upon: so we, in weakness, may take hold of God our strength.

Feel too sick to think. *One* knows, pities,
and loves. "When my spirit was overwhelmed within me, then Thou knewest my

6

path." Amid all my pain, my heart is resting upon Infinite Love. The still small voice
whispers often, " Be still, and know that I am
God."

Received a letter from M—— to-day. The
tone was very sad, and she expressed solici-
tude with regard to me ; but " I have received
good at the hand of the Lord, and shall I not
receive evil ? " My own heart is calm and
still, in harmony with the outer world. Feel
alone, — such perfect heart-solitude ! but I
am only continuing with Jesus. He was like
a pelican of the wilderness, and an owl of the
desert.

The promise, " According to thy day, so shall
thy strength be," has been fully verified, physically and spiritually. I have been able, in
my weakness, to attend to all that was needful ;

and when remarks were made, causing the heart
to bleed, God bent tenderly over me, and whispered, "I have torn, and will heal; I have
smitten, and will bind up."

Have felt calm to-day. My portion from
the divine Word was, "Help me, O Lord! for
I am weak; strengthen me according to thy
word." "My strength shall be made perfect
in weakness." Resting in God! All is well.
Though hope is deferred long, the heart does
not grow sick; for it rests upon the immutable
will of God.

Life has many burdens, I know ; but strength
equal to our burden counteracts the pressure.
Do you think we fully appreciate this idea of
equality in the divine life? If we did, life
would have less crosses. Lest I should lose

the beautiful idea, I have written down the formula, —

Strength = to Burden.

These have been beautiful weeks, — these seven that I have lain so sweetly in the arms of Jesus. Am perfectly happy still: no anxious thought disturbs the deep calm of my soul. Since I am prostrated, and can do nothing myself, it seems so easy to let God do all! I have never lost the power of that thought that was whispered to me by the Spirit that last night we were together: " God loves you better than you can love yourself; your interests are as dear to him as to you: wait and trust." I hope I may never be left again to doubt the love and care of my Father, lest I again be accused with, " O ye of little faith ! wherefore didst thou doubt ? "

Oh these precious sick-room hours with Jesus! The place seems to me like the very vestibule of glory. Such sweet manifestations of the divine presence! — such holy communings in the night-watches, when feverish and restless! Surely He giveth his beloved rest.

I have not felt at all good of late. It has been so long since I have been with those that are deeply devoted, so long since I have had the soul-inspiring influence of meetings, that I seem to be getting careless and languid in my feelings. But no matter how much earthly aid we have: it is Christ, after all, that we need. Precious Jesus! How wretched I should be without him! and yet how cold is my love!

> " Cold in my warmest vows, — vain my truest;
> Thoughts of a lingering hour, —
> Our lips repeat them, our hearts forget them."

Oh! may my faith rise and stretch her wings, taking hold of the promises of God, that joy may abound, and peace flow like a river!

How' tenderly Jesus draws me to himself, and whispers, "I have betrothed thee unto me in righteousness"! Sweet Jesus! precious, loving Saviour! infinite condescension! Yet I do believe thou art mine, and I am thine. Never did I love thee as I do now; and yet how weak my love, compared with thine! Oh for a more perfect union with thyself, and a nature more assimilated to thy own!

"How precious are thy thoughts unto me, O God! how great is the sum of them!" My soul feeds upon the divine Word! How like crumbs are portions dealt out to us from time to time as we need them! "The Lord is thy keeper; the Lord is thy shade upon

thy right hand." " They shall prosper that
love thee." ' How can I doubt, though clouds
and darkness are round about ? I do love my
God : hence " no evil can befall me."

I congratulate you on the weary, prostrated
condition of which you write ; for the abundance of grace, and the rich experience that
attends suffering, are so desirable, that I ever
feel that I would be congratulated instead of
pitied. And then God's love to his suffering
ones is so peculiarly tender ! " He shall gently
lead those that are with young ; " i. e., any
special burden or weakness. Always when
I am suffering intensely, or more especially
after the keenness of the suffering is past,
and I lie weak and prostrated, then the silvery
accents of the voice of Christ are heard,
breaking the stillness of my sick-room, and
saying, " I will gather the lambs with my arm,

and carry them in my bosom." Faith makes the promise mine. I am a weak lamb. He takes me up in his arms, and carries me over the rough places of my suffering; requiring nothing of me but to be still, and rest upon his bosom. The one idea, that infinite arms are holding me, is such a vivid soul-realization, such an actuality, that I seem to have no fears or wants. I only rest, and am satisfied.

My nature is confiding. It is almost as easy for me to lean my head on Jesus' breast, and believe that he loves me, as it was for the beloved disciple. When I view my heart so deformed and corrupt, in my utter nothingness and unloveliness, I am so wretched, that the heart instinctively reaches out for something; and where could I go but to Jesus? I run to him, and so confidingly too, that he throws over my pollution his own glorious robe of righteousness. He washes away every stain in his own precious blood; and then it seems the Father cannot help loving me, when he sees the seal of the covenant upon the soul redeemed and made white. I once felt afraid of God, and would hide myself in Christ, and not take my thoughts from him; but now Christ has revealed God to me, not as a Being of absolute holiness and justice alone, but as God the Father. There is tenderness in the very term. Then why approach God so timidly, with so little confidence? We surely take the very way Jesus told us: "No man cometh unto the Father but by me." "I am the door: by me if any man enter in, he shall be saved." How positive! "Lord, I believe."

I feel so happy and trusting just now, and take so much comfort in literally looking unto

Jesus! Temptation and sin so quickly lose power! One look suffices to overcome. Trials come thick and fast; many things are against me : but the one precious thought, that there is an ever-present Jesus, sufficeth.

How sweetly the words of Jesus fell upon my heart to-day!" — "I will pray the Father for thee." Jesus praying for *me*, — always pleading my cause to the Father! Oh wondrous thought! Take thou hold of it, my soul, and be strong.

Yesterday, while reading Psalm cv., my faith looked up to the Mighty One who could cause water to gush forth from the rock ; and kneeling beside my bed, where so many prayers have been offered, I cried, " If it be possible, restore dear M—— to health, that she may engage actively in Thy service."

Jesus is interceding for you and for me. I have left the petition in His hands who is faithful. I rest upon His word, which is my delight.

Wearisome days and nights are appointed now ; but by the eye of faith do I see God. " I know that my Redeemer lives," — lives to pity, love, and pray for me.

> " God is love, I know, I feel :
> Jesus weeps and loves me still."

You ask, dear sister, if it is well with me. It is well. My faith still clings to that blessed Saviour who has never yet forsaken me, and who has said, " Lo, I am with you alway." While leaning on the arm of my Beloved, I fear no evil. Clinging to him, borne by him, I can safely glide across the dark and narrow stream, lighted by the radiance of his own glory, and rise triumphantly as he, our Redeemer, has risen.

Oh blessed assurance! God knoweth best. And soon this assurance shall infinitely outstretch that resulting from faith, which is the evidence of things not seen; for, being like Him, "we shall see Him as he is." Then these trials, which by faith "work out for us a far more exceeding and eternal weight of glory," shall, as troubles, sink into the utmost insignificance; but, as blessings, shall magnify the grace and tender love of our Father in heaven. And this time is not surely far away. I feel it more and more each succeeding day; and my heart leaps with gladness as I grasp more fondly the glorious promise, "He that overcometh, the same shall be clothed in white raiment; and I will not blot his name out of the book of life."

Mother M—— was in. Oh, she is so fully controlled by the Spirit! Her face bears the image of the heavenly, and beams with a holy light. I can talk with her almost as with Christ. How sweet to interchange thoughts with Christ's little ones, — those who bear the appellation, "The disciple whom Jesus loved"!

As in weakness and pain I looked down the vista of the past, dwelt upon the present, with hopes crushed, plans foiled, and health gone, and, tearing away the veil, gazed out into the darkness of the future, I became restless and discontented, and cried out, "Why hath the Lord led me thus?" And, in a moment, I was conscious of letting go my hold of Christ. My feet slipped from their firm foundation. I sank down, down. Oh, it was fearful! I realized as never before the true source of my strength, and how I had been kept from sinking in all the struggle of life. I did not sink when all my earth-props were removed, because I clung to Christ; but now I doubted, and Christ was gone. With what eagerness of soul I ran back to my offended Lord, and, with tears of penitence, fell upon his bosom! Oh sweet embrace!— home of the soul, how sweet! God directed me to this word of inspiration, "I have led thee these forty years;" which opened my eyes, and showed me that it was in love and tenderness that he had thus dealt with me. Patient, infinite love! I was humbled and satisfied. Thenceforth I have loved my cross; for it is the way to the heavenly home and the crowned band. God knoweth best. Trusting, "I hold still."

I know I shall reach the heights and depths

of Jesus' love, and that soon. I shall be the
Lord's fully and entirely. There are seasons
when I feel that I am fully consecrated; but
faith trembles. As the little child at first cannot bear its own weight, but totters and falls,
so I stagger in the way. But I will press on.
Strength will come, I know, bringing rest and
peace.

Is it not sweet to say, away down deep in
the heart, " Thy will be done"? Please, do not
feel solicitous. I have found the way to my
Father's bank, and receive all needed supplies.
I have only to tell him my needs, and he answers while I am yet speaking: " They that
trust in the Lord shall want no good thing."

Very deep and dark are the waters over
which I am now passing. While I keep my eye
steadily fixed upon Christ, my tread is firm, my

footing sure. I go forth with God-like strength and calmness. But, if for a moment I look down to the billows raging about me, my strength wanes; I sink in deep waters. Clinging, clinging to Christ, I am safe. Each turn of the racking wheel but extracts a more emphatic " Thy will be done." Each added trial but calls forth a fuller, louder song, " Holy, holy, holy Lord God Almighty ! " Each severe attack of suffering seems to hew off one more rough corner of my human nature, and make me more perfectly in the image of my Divine Master. Oh ! when shall I be like him ? when shall I fully reflect his image ? I know my trials are needed, and not one redundant pang will my Father give me.

As I was thinking yesterday how lonely it would be among entire strangers, the thought flashed through my mind, I shall know one, —

Jesus. My Jesus will be there. The thought satisfied me. It was enough. My happy heart bounded to his infinite embrace. I was soothed and comforted with the whisperings of my Beloved, " I will never leave thee nor forsake thee."

I love my cross; my pains are sweet; for Christ gives me the whole of himself to bear them with. I am very sure God has a design in all that he has appointed.

> "Its end may come, and will to-morrow,
> When God has done his work in me."

How mysterious are the ways of God! " But what to us is shadow, to him is day; and the end thereof he knoweth."

" Be not weary in well-doing; for in due season ye shall reap, if ye faint not. I will not

7

leave you comfortless. Be strong, and of good courage; fear not, neither be afraid of them: for the Lord thy God, he it is that doth go with thee; he will not fail thee, nor forsake thee." Thank God for this strong tower of defence!

GOD'S SPARROW.

Luke xii. 6, 7.

I wake with morning's freshness to find the prom-
 ise true, —
 He giveth his beloved —
 His wearied and beloved —
Sleep, falling on the drooping lids like purple
 evening-dew.

I join the mighty chorus; but gentle is my lay:
 For quivering is the harp-string —
 The sorrow-tensioned harp-string —
That teemeth with its music from morn till clos-
 ing day.

I pray the heavenly Father my daily need supply,
  And send the angel-raven —
  Good old Elijah's raven —
To give me earthly manna when for my bread I cry.

In days of olden story, the angels walked abroad,
  With blessings for the holy, —
  The faithful and the holy, —
Who bore upon the door-posts the sprinklings of
    their Lord.

God now has earthly angels, who hear the still
    small voice,
  And, with their well-filled baskets, —
  Their dantily-filled baskets, —
Go forth to bless the humble, and make the heart
    rejoice.

By them my daily portion is meted out to me;
  For I'm an humble sparrow, —
  A weakly, trusting sparrow, —
Whose wings are clipped on purpose, providing
    care to see.

Ay, oft our heavenly blessings are masked in
Sorrow's shroud.
What seem but heavy burdens
Are richly-freighted guerdons,
While steadily the sunbeam is fluttering in the
cloud.

It needs a holy vision to pierce through God's
intent;
A lofty faith to guide us
In all that may betide us
While, through these darkly windings, our weary
steps are bent.

With faith in God's dear promise, I'll love the
appointed way;
Not anxious for the morrow, —
The misty, veiled morrow, —
But singing in my sorrow,
God careth for the sparrow, with each returning
day.

Chap. III.   Page 101.

III.

SELF-CONSECRATION.

YOUR request for mutual prayer, upon the all-important subject of entire consecration, makes me feel strangely. It seems to bring the question to a point where I must decide it at once. Yet how can I? I believe fully, firmly, in perfect love; but can *I* be holy?

When I become thus personal, the mind gets into a whirl; for there is so much to be overcome, — so much pride, such desires to be humbled, and yet such a dread of being humbled!

How much there is in and around us to prevent a holy life! How the serpent of sin peers up his ugly head, and leers and laughs, and twines himself about us, till we are bound hand and foot, and the very life in us dies!

Yet, God helping me, I, too, will cry, " Crucify me, crucify me ! "

> "I can but perish if I go:
> I am resolved to try."

You query if I have any of those trials peculiar to helpless invalids. Ah, dear! I long to tell you. I try to keep ever before me the idea of "bearing all things, enduring all things," and, like Jesus, to open not my mouth.

Am so glad I thus rigidly disciplined myself

when strong! for it is so much easier now in my weakness!

When I am comfortable, I am surprised at my unmoved, untroubled state of feeling; but, when weak from constant suffering, the struggle is more severe. But nerves, too, must be taught patience. Religion can do it: it does do it. Thank God!

I wonder that all Christians are not holy. They must be; they must be! Oh the great chasm between Jesus and the soul! When will the soul startle into new life?

The week is overpast; but I am nearer heaven. Precious have been its privileges, drawing my heart upward. If consecration, and living solely in looking to Jesus, will make a soul "whiter than snow," I trust to be pure in heart.

I feel so quiet and calm, and keep looking upward! and it is easier now to discern the dividing-line between temptation and sin. I would not be less harsh with myself; but I find, on closest scrutiny, that sometimes I may stumble, and not sin.

I commenced this month to fast every Thursday morning, and to spend two or three hours alone with God in heart-searching, careful Bible-study, and prayer. I do enjoy the season very much, and am conscious of rapid spiritual growth. I am guarding myself against over-eating, knowing that I often eat more than nature demands, simply to gratify appetite. I consider it to be wrong, as it injures the stomach, and oppresses the mind, preventing a lively exercise of faith. I can enjoy prayer much better after a light meal: hence, when I have eaten plentifully of the first course, I deny myself of dessert, however tempting it may be. I am thus benefited in a twofold sense, — health is promoted, and self crucified.

One after another of my human feelings is crucified ; self is gradually dying ; Jesus is all.

I find my conscience becoming tender upon various matters, — eating, drinking, convers- ing, &c. The idea might seem a narrow one to many, simply a scrupulous notion ; but, to the advanced Christian, they become matters of importance. I love these gentle sugges- tions of the Spirit with reference to a close walk. I was visiting a short time since, of an evening, in the family of a friend. There was

a painful want of sociability ; and, in my at-
tempt to remove it, I became too loquacious.
On returning, I felt dissatisfied. In my effort
to make myself agreeable, I had not every
moment kept myself under the control of the
Holy Spirit. And yet it was not the character of my words, but the amount of talking,
that I felt did not quite please my heavenly
Father. " Let no corrupt communication pro-
ceed out of your mouth ; but that which is
good to the use of edifying, that it may minis-
ter grace unto the hearers."

I find it is better to think of Christ than to
dwell upon imperfect, erring, stumbling self.
I am praying that self may be crushed out, —
that it may die. When self dies, then Christ
is all. Not my own, not my own, but His
who bought me with his blood, and sprinkles
that cleansing blood continually.

The soul seems to have grown sensitive since Thursday. Light expressions from others, or any thing not strictly holy, has given me pain, causing the soul to shrink, just as the plant folds up at the slightest touch of the finger. Jesus was not pleased at such, and I want to be just like him in every thing.

God teaches us our lessons one by one, as we are able to receive them. I am conscious, in the discipline I am now receiving, God is teaching me unselfishness. How much I want this ruling evil rooted out of my heart, that I may love to do for others as well as myself!

When I find myself more than usually in earnest to become perfected in any of the Christian graces, I have increased opportunities given me to exercise them, and in a greater degree. I have felt these little trials to be so needful, that I have almost regarded the authors of them as blameless, and suffering on my account.

I am praying to be humbled. God is answering my prayer, and crumbling my pride. Yet will I pray, " Humble me to the very dust ! " The severest trial for months came to me Saturday. But I regard it in answer to prayer; for it was a humbling trial, — one that did me much good. God knows best: I can endure what he sends.

Trials affect us in proportion to the strength we have. When very weak physically, little things annoy me ; but I find in the precious Word an antidote full and efficient: " Be strong in the grace that is in Christ."

I am strangely perverse sometimes; but

Jesus is so kind, that my heart swells in tenderness, and I keep loving him, notwithstanding my waywardness and many imperfections.

Have been trying very hard this week to carry out the perfect rule of Christ, and do by others as I would like to be done by.

The Holy Spirit taught me I had been unwilling to bear this trial. Had it been sickness, I should have at once recognized God's will; but this was a trial so entirely new, that, for the time, I forgot that I might cast even this burden upon the Lord.

But, as faith took hold upon God, " a present help," a flood of glory, came and swept away my sadness, and wafted my soul into the haven of God's great, loving bosom; and, as I rested there, I was enabled to look back upon the great deep, and see how God had led me. Oh wondrous love!

The trial is not removed; but "grace sufficient" makes the burden light, and all is well.

Have felt so dissatisfied with myself of late! There seems no good thing in me. I commit errors in all my attempts to do good, and my life seems a failure.

How solemn a thing to live! God grant wisdom and a sanctified judgment! for I know not the way in which I should go.

Watch and pray. If we do this, we shall be kept from fretting and chafing under the ordinary perplexities of life. If we are conquered by our human feelings, in what do we differ from the world? "Do not the publicans the same?" It has been truly said, "The Christian life is constant warfare, constant victory."

On making a proposition, and receiving no answer of sympathy, the question occurred, " Will it always be thus, as it ever has been, that these finer feelings of the heart must be so little appreciated ? " And the answer came, " Not there, not there, my child ! "

So many little heart-trials of late ! But instead of asking to have them lessened, or my trials removed, I have prayed for grace to bear them in the meek, loving spirit of Jesus, " who was oppressed and afflicted, yet he opened not his mouth."

The poor heart, like the roe heated in the chase, pants for God, the living God. "When shall I come and appear before God ? " How repeatedly we feel the deep incisions of the pruning-knife, and hear the Master saying,

"Every branch that beareth fruit, I purge it, that it may bring forth more fruit "!

Yet I would be constant and obedient, though all be taken from me; for my Lord, "though he were a Son, yet learned he obedience by the things which he suffered ; and, being made perfect, he is the author of salvation unto all them that obey him."

God has placed you just where you are : he has appointed you your present duties, and subjected you to your present trials. Why so ? It is surely not as a means of punishment ; for he does not "willingly grieve or afflict the children of men."

He studies our happiness as well as our best good : hence he must be designing this discipline ultimately, even in this life, for your good and happiness. Now, what is the lesson to be learned ?

Most emphatically, long-suffering, patience, unselfishness. You are daily praying for these graces in perfection; and it is only in the exercise of your own powers, with the use of God's grace, that this can be accomplished.

Yes, this discipline comes in answer to prayer. It is the only way, undoubtedly, that we could be perfected; and, though the flesh cries out hard for life, the spirit prays that it may fully die.

Have been much tempted in respect to my inefficiency. Every thing I do seems so unsatisfactory! Long and earnestly have I prayed for release; and, thank God! victory has come at last.

I had a sweet realization of Jesus stooping down, and drawing me away from the coils of

8

the enemy.   What condescension! Christ, the
High and Holy, stooping for such as me!

> " Saviour, keep me near thy side ;
>   Let thy counsels be my guide ;
>   Never let me from thee rove ;
>   Sweetly draw me by thy love."

Am loosing my grasp of earthly things, and
staying my heart more steadily upon God.

When storms of sorrow rise, he calms the
troubled waters of the soul ; and I realize the
sweet verification of the promise, " Great
peace have they that love Thy law ; and
nothing shall offend them."

Some have been disposed to find fault with
the course I have pursued ; but I have felt
it an honor to be reproached for Christ while
securely I have been hid beneath the almighty
wing.   Glory to Jesus for victory! I am

learning many lessons of Jesus, my blessed teacher. He is so patient, while I am so slow and hard to learn ! Dying daily ! — thou. dear Lord, knowest the sorrows of this death.

In some positions, it seems to take all the energy of our moral nature to stem opposing influences ; hence we cannot at the time realize that we are making progress in the divine life : but, when our surroundings are more favorable, we find the resistance to stem the tide of earthliness has so strengthened our Christian character, and developed moral energy, that, for a time, it seems so easy to " run the Christain race with patience."

In every situation, we are dependent upon ourselves in " working out our salvation ; " while always we need a strong reliance upon the God of strength.

Had a severe struggle with the Enemy last
evening. He has too long made me a slave
to my extreme sensitiveness; and I resolved
I would break away from its thraldom, and
gain a lasting victory. For an hour I wrestled
with God in prayer. The struggle was great.
It was so hard to nail the darling objects of
my love and pride to the cross, and calmly
watch them die! But thank God, who giveth
us victory through Jesus Christ our Lord!
I rose a conqueror; and, as I let go my hold
of earthly objects, I sank fully into God. A
holy indifference pervaded my heart to every
thing of earth; and for a long time I walked
my room in "perfect peace," whispering
praises to God and the Lamb, who hath redeemed us, and washed us in his own precious
blood.

How few understand us! and none so fully

as Jesus. How many, many trials we have, that, being both relative and absolute in character, we cannot seem to speak of to any one, lest we seem to be finding fault, or to make the faults of others too prominent! which we do not like to do, as it would seem uncharitable; and we would avoid the very appearance of evil. . . .

We alone feel the trial, and we alone must bear it silently. And yet not alone; for Jesus feels every sorrow his children bear. Does not his great heart yearn pityingly over us in our silent woe ? . . .

Precious Jesus! let us never grieve thee by a lack of confidence, but ever bring all, all to thee !

Have in two or three instances to-day tried to keep God's words; but in each case it was so unsatisfactory to self, that, if any good was done, it must have been all of God. . . .

I notice God has been especially leading me thus of late; but I would hold still, and let God slay self. When I hold up the cross, I would have that the only attraction.

My heart condemns me for being so far from the " highway of holiness." I seem to stand in the way of God's will. Break, my hard heart, and yield to Him who waits to be gracious! I seem to yield a little at a time, by degrees: but my conscience tells me all should go at once; every thing should be swept away.

Shall I hold out stubborn, and souls be lost? Remove me, my Saviour, from the way, and let the tide of thy love sweep on and melt souls!

You ask if our temptations are less in strength and number after sanctification. Our

temptations arise from three sources, — the
world, the flesh, and the Devil. Those aris-
ing from the world and the flesh are less
after the heart is fully sanctified, because we
are then " dead to the world, " — dead to its
fashions, its customs, its maxims, and pleas-
ures. . . .

The world stands in contrast with heaven ;
and it appears so very insignificant, that few
temptations arise from that source. . . .

Again : the flesh is crucified with the affections and lusts, and the whole tide of our
feelings and desires is changed. The things
we once loved, now we hate ; and the things
we once hated, now we love : so that the tide
of temptation from this source, which has so
readily overcome us before, is now rolled
back. . . .

But, so long as the Christian remains in the
world, so long will he be subject to the as-

saults of the Devil. We shall never be more pure, more fully sanctified, than our blessed Master; and yet how strong and how numerous were his temptations !

It is the great aim of the Adversary to prevent us from getting to heaven: and the more earnest we are in striving to reach the heavenly goal, the more diligent we are in prosecuting our journey, the more diligent is the great Enemy of our souls ; so that the sanctified heart finds his assaults increased in strength and number.

Wept bitterly to-day over my selfish heart. There are times when I have to struggle very hard to deny myself, and love my neighbor as I would be loved. O unselfishness, thou art a jewel ! When shall I have thee in full possession ? " He that overcometh will I make a pillar in the temple of my God, and he shall go no more out; and I will write upon him my new name."

Dr. R——, in his prayer this morning, asked that we might bid a " God-speed " to every one that could do better, appear better, and learn better, than ourselves. A hearty response to this welled up from my soul. . . .

Oh, how I long to have the root of envy and pride fully eradicated from my heart! . . .

It will be pleasant to reach heaven, because we are so sure of being free from all evil there.

Have been looking steadily upward. My attention has been called to " For ye have need of patience ; " and I have had to manufacture so much to-day, as from time to time little careless words have been dropped ! How comforting, in all these heart-trials, to know Jesus is afflicted !

Feel deeply humble. Am so unlike Christ! and yet I dare not look at self, but keep looking to the Lamb of God. One look of penitence and faith to Him, our present Saviour, is worth more than hours of self-abasement, or years of trying to make one's self better.

Have felt especially the importance of keeping "my mouth with a bridle while the wicked are before me."

> "Speak well of all :
> 'Twill be a medicine to thy own heart."

My heart seems languid in its spiritual pulsation, still and emotionless. Have deep and abasing views of self; but it makes the fulness of Christ and his all-sufficiency more apparent. Would that I could feel it more! but non-feeling is controlled by God, as well as feeling.

I would lie passive as clay in the hands of the potter. It is not by emotion, but by faith, we stand.

I see in Christ an infinite store, all for me; but when shall I attain to it? My longing soul is impatient at this snail-pace movement heavenward. I wonder I do not, as on the wings of thought, leave all that looks toward sin, or has any affinity for it, and seek the most intimate communion with Christ. I lean too much upon self, too little upon the all-sufficient One, who feeds the hungry soul with fatness.

"Nearer, my God, to thee; nearer to thee!"

I am trying not to be influenced so much by emotion; not to study experience so much, but Christ more. He is the grand model by which I would shape my inner life: upon his pure and faultless life would I ever keep my eye fixed. Precious Christ! Can it be that I may be "changed into the same image, from glory to glory, even as by the Spirit of the Lord"?

How responsible the life of a Christian! How much depends upon his acts, looks, and words! The thought has impressed me strongly of late.

I must walk carefully, so that poor souls may not become bewildered, and wonder if there is a reality in what the Christian professes.

"I FEAR I AM TOO HAPPY."

This joy that now my being thrills,
　I fear its potent sway;
For this is earth, where purest joy
　Lasts only for a day,

And then the midnight clouds of gloom
Are blown athwart our way.

This casket with a priceless gem —
A loving, human heart,
On which to lean when weak and lone
In all life's sterner part —
Is a gift so dear, I fear too soon
Will come the arrow's dart.

I would not of this heavenly gift
An earthly idol make,
But bring it to the shrine above,
And love it for Christ's sake;
For He who giveth every gift
. Has the same power to take.

But daily does my prayer ascend
That I may purer be;
And, as God's chosen ones are led
In ways they cannot see,

I tremble, lest my darling prop
　　May be removed from me.

God's will be done!   I cannot tell
　　What shadows dark may fall;
But, sure his love will seek my good,
　　I leave the future's pall,
And, trusting, work with busy hands
　　To meet the present call.

His thoughts are higher than our own;
　　His ways are just and right:
And though he goeth forth in clouds,
　　Girded with power and might,
Yet gold and purple is his garb,
　　When we can see aright.

Saviour all pure and glorious,
　　I bring my gem to thee;
Burnish and fit it for thy crown,
　　My dear beloved and me:
And, when our work is finished here,
　　Bring us thy face to see!

IV.

CROSS-BEARING.

YES, I often think of a "home in heaven." The very thought fills my soul with rapture. When the time comes for me to go home, if strength is given, I shall shout aloud for joy. But I feel the time is not yet.

I am like the man sent by his government to some foreign country to transact business of great importance. In that distant clime, he thinks of his own dear native land; and that sunny spot, his own sweet home: and there come ardent longings for the dear ones he has left behind.

But he remembers the duty he owes to his country, the trust which has been committed to him; and though he loves his home so well, yet he would not return to it one moment before his work is done.

Thus have I a work, a great work, to do; and though I love to think of home and rest, and the loved who are gone before, waiting to -welcome me on the bright shore; though

"I would not live alway away from my God," —

yet I would live, be my lot ever so hard, my sufferings ever so great, till I can say with my blessed Master, "I have finished the work Thou gavest me to do."

Whatever good we do, small though it be, has a reflex influence upon ourselves. Giving, we receive; teaching, we learn. "It is more blessed to give than to receive," saith the Master.

On reading your letter, I longed to be near you, that I might, by the assistance of God, stay up your hands. My heart ached for you as I read of your toiling long and earnestly in the vineyard; and when the hopes you had so long cherished were about to be realized, that then you should have such a trial of your faith! . . . I wonder not that the tears would come, and that tired nature almost sank to the earth. Oh! when we try with all our strength to labor for those around us; when we get a view of the imminent danger of those out of Christ; when we realize the great responsibility resting upon the followers of Christ, and yet see them so unwilling to come up to the help of the Lord

against the mighty,—oh! then, how we fly
to the bosom of Jesus, and there pour out our
sorrows! for we are sure of finding sympathy
in him if all other sources fail.   Dear Saviour,
let us rest in thy arms from the conflict a
little season, that we may gather strength for
the great work thou hast given us to do.

Tried to breathe the name of Jesus to a poor
sinner very near his end.   He was so sick, it
seemed difficult for him to grasp the idea of
a Saviour by faith.   Poor soul! if he, in health,
had been obedient, now he could sing,—

> "Jesus! the name that charms our fears,
> That bids our sorrows cease."

Father, have mercy!—only that can save
from guilt and sin.

When I speak to my school upon the subject of religion, I am surprised to see how

much tenderness they exhibit. They are nearly. all moved to tears. But I know God is the same, whatever the instrument. . . .

Oh that I may be the vessel of the Lord to bear the water of life to these precious spirits!

Felt directed to speak a word of cheer to Miss R. ; but she remarked, " I am in a hurry." I replied, " I will detain you but a moment;" and then whispered, " I am praying for you." God smiled; but I could not help thinking, How earthly! Nothing quite to our taste here, but always something unsatisfactory, — just enough to turn our thoughts Godward.

No: my work is not yet done. If so, why this constant outreaching and earnestness of soul, this intensity of feeling, and love for sinners? I sometimes feel that I must rise

up, and go out and save that " other " one left
upon the wreck of sin and death.

As I receive more of God, my love for the
lost increases ; and I so long to bear the water
of life to earth's poor thirsty children!

How many were hurried into eternity by
that sad typhoon ! God hasten the time when
a " nation shall be born in a day " !

I am obliged to leave school, and go home.
Once, on such a disappointment, I should have
longed for my heavenly home ; but I do not
feel those impatient longings now. . . .

My prayer is, " Cut me not off in the midst
of my days, but spare me yet to labor in the
vineyard of my Master."

Am so tired! but God giveth his beloved
rest. Find so much to keep the mind on the
stretch ! But I love to toil for Christ. " It

matters not whether crowned or crownless,"
since he is glorified, and God's will is done.

Have been conversing with Brother V——
upon the deep things of God, and feel that it
has been of mutual profit. Had the sweet consciousness that God was using me as his own
chosen vessel, and that the Holy Spirit was
controlling every word and thought. . . .

It is painfully sad that so much of our religion consists of theory, and that we have
so little of the power of godliness. . . .

Oh that men would take hold upon God,
carrying him into their entire lives ! Only
thus can we be a power to move the world.

There seems to be danger of making the
cross of Christ a boast. Think I am less ex-
posed to that temptation here than in some
places. . . .

The fulness that dwells in the Godhead bodily seems to be so little appreciated by the mass of Christians, that when I speak of Jesus, or any heart-experience, I seem to have to do it in obedience to the command, " Let your light so shine before men, that they may see your good works, and glorify your Father which is in heaven." . . .

God smiles sweetly; and that satisfies me. Jesus was not understood, even by his own disciples: so are we comparative strangers, though journeying together as the children of a King.

Have been trying to lead J—— to Jesus. Feel so very happy in the work of raising fallen mortals up to Christ the crucified! He smiles upon my weak endeavors, making the burden light. . . .

Oh wondrous privilege, to co-operate with Divinity in saving a lost world!

We have had the news of dear L.'s death.
My first thought was of his poor soul : then
came the thought, "I did what I could."
It was some comfort to me ; but I cannot
know whether it proved good to him or not.
Earnestly did I labor for him when he was
under my care ; and nightly, during his ab-
sence, have I brought him to the altar of
God. Would that I could know he looked to
the Lamb of God in those last hours of life !
but I cannot till that great day that shall dis-
close the secrets of men, and bring to light
the hidden things of darkness.

I am having a new cross to bear, and have
need of peculiar strength. One by one do
earthly sources fail, till sometimes it seems
we have none but Jesus left. With him I
will walk the rugged way, that I may share
his glory hereafter.

"Father, I thank thee for the cross
So kindly to me given,
To make me think the less of earth,
And more of thee and heaven."

I——— intends to sail to-morrow. What can I say to him about his unsaved soul? Will write a letter, and put it with the home-parcel, to be found when he is away. Spirit Divine, attend the word, and fix his roving heart on God and heaven!

At the prayer-meeting last evening, the house was filled. Souls were hungering for the bread of life; but there seemed to be no one to feed them. . . .

I could not let the evening pass in silence, knowing I should meet those souls at the judgment. I talked, prayed, and sung, as the Spirit gave utterance. Hearts were moved, and eyes filled with tears, as boldly I stood up for Jesus, and spoke of the power of his love.

Glorious grace, that restores the soul to union with Christ, and enables us to be co-workers with him in the salvation of the world! Go on in thy holy work, and labor of love; for "they that go forth weeping, bearing precious seed, shall doubtless come again with rejoicing, bringing their sheaves with them."

"I have given all for Jesus;
　　　　　Henceforth, then,
It matters not if storm or sunshine be
My earthly lot, bitter or sweet my cup:
I only pray, God fit me for the work,
God make me holy, and my spirit nerve
For the stern hour of strife!"

God, in his infinite wisdom, permits some

of his children to labor in his vineyard, but never to see the fruit of their labors till heaven's light dawns upon them. On earth they must toil on, only upheld by the sure promise, — the seed will spring up, and God will be glorified, though they see *it* not. . . .

Doubtless much of your labor as a teacher must be thus wrought; but when, in our utter weakness, we are tempted to discouragement and doubt, we will remember that not one prayer from the truly trusting heart falls upon the divine ear unheeded.

Since I commenced to write, two little black boys came in to see me. One has just become a Christian : the other desires to be. I had a sweet season with them, and felt my own heart burn within me as I pointed them to the spotless Lamb for sinners slain. . . .

How happy I am in this holy work of crying, "Behold, behold, the Lamb!"

New duties to-day. Thus are they appointed, while we obey the injunction, to deny ourselves daily, and take up the cross, and follow Christ.

> "One by one thy duties wait thee;
> Let thy whole strength go to each :
> Let no future dreams elate thee;
> Learn thou first what these can teach."

I love the ambition of Cæsar and Napoleon, though unsanctified; and do not wonder that Alexander wept that he had not another world to conquer. I would be thus ambitious for God and his cause. Oh for a zeal that will urge us on to the steady contest till the Enemy be conquered, and we win a crown brilliant with immortal gems !

This place, where I have spent so many happy and profitable hours, seems very dear to me; but, as I leave it, it is sweet to think I am going forth to labor for a good Master, and in a glorious cause. . . .

When I think of my Saviour's love, how much he endured and suffered for me, I feel that no sacrifice is too much, no labor too great, for Him who merits all my love.

It seems sometimes strange to me that every one is not in earnest, doing with their might what their hands find to do. . . . There is so much to be done, and so short a time in which to do it! Eternity, eternity, eternity! and only a brief hour to make ready for it!

> "Every hour that fleets so slowly
> Has its task to do or bear:
> Luminous the crown, and holy,
> If thou set each gem with care."

Have been laboring with A——. Oh that he could enter into this blessed rest of faith! It keeps the heart so calm and peaceful, while all may be tumult without!

"If all the world my Saviour knew,
    Sure all the world would love him too."

I do love the cross. There is such a glory surrounding it, that, when I draw near to take it up, my soul is permeated and filled unutterably full of glory and of God. Then is the cross a delight, and no burden. Glorious grace, that can give worms like us such holy boldness!

Have been conversing with Mr. W——. I hope none of us will set our standard of piety so low as to miss of heaven.

How sad it would be to hear the Judge say, "I never knew you"!

"Oh, what a glorious record had the angels of me kept,
    Had I done instead of doubted, had I warred instead of
        wept."

Dear A—— has at last entered into rest. She was powerfully wrought upon by the Spirit in the female prayer-meeting; and, when we returned home, we bowed together till a late hour, pleading for mercy. When she did lay herself helpless at the foot of the cross, peace filled her heart, and a divine light rested upon her countenance.

Sweet was the season of rejoicing; and heaven echoed with the glad cry, "Another soul is born of God!" May she ever be thine, O God! All glory to the bleeding Lamb! Sinners are coming home!

The year has passed, freighted with many mercies to me. I rejoice that I have been counted worthy to labor in the vineyard. Have learned many lessons at the cross, and gained many victories over self.

Would have my whole will swallowed up in the divine; then can I go forth to do battle for the Lord unto certain victory.

"Two golden hours, each set with a jewel of sixty minutes. No reward is offered; for they are lost, — irrevocably lost!"

This thought has roused every energy of my being. Time, though precious, is flying; souls are being lost; and I must rest not by the way, but work, work.

A missionary association is said to have adopted this device, found on an ancient medal, which represented a bullock standing between a plough and an altar, with this inscription, "Ready for either, — ready for toil or for sacrifice."

Exalting thought! Whatever my mission, whether toil or suffering, I would ever say, " Ready for either."

> " Nearer the port by every wave.
>   Be strong, my heart! my soul, be brave!
>   Theirs the gain who suffer loss ;
>   Theirs the crown who bear the cross."

The burden of souls rests heavily upon me. I. want to bear the water of life to every one I meet. So did the blessed Christ, when he stood on that great day of the feast, and cried, " If any man thirst, let him come unto me and drink."

1 fear I have too much overlooked the little opportunities for usefulness in my ardent desire to do some great work ; but I am resolved to do so no longer. It is the little things that make up life. A smile, a tear, a

tender word of love, may do so much to lighten heavy burdens!

If I am cut off from the path in which my ambition would lead me, I will faithfully study the little opportunities of doing good, and cheerfully perform my work therein.

Controlled by the Holy Spirit, clothed in Christ's righteousness, we may be a living power, in whatever capacity we move or act.

Have realized God "a present help" in carrying out my resolution to be more active in spiritual labor in school. Have felt so happy in doing little errands for the Lord!

Duty done brings its own sure reward. Help I every moment need, that I may let no opportunity of usefulness slip.

"Do with thy might whatsoever thy hand

10

findeth to do" has been reiterated in my hearing by the Holy Spirit, till I have seemed to regard earth as one broad field for action, where there is no room or time for one idle spectator.

Have been filling up my spare moments in conversing with sinners. Wrote a note of spiritual encouragement to Miss D., for which she seemed very grateful. God is beautifully leading her up the shining way.

Have been greatly blessed in bearing the cross of late. I am surprised that we have so much trembling and fear, when the promises are so full and sufficient. "They that wait upon the Lord shall renew their strength; they shall mount up with wings as eagles; they shall run, and not be weary; and they shall walk, and not faint."

Am holding a little prayer-meeting for the children. There is a deep interest; and several have sought and found Jesus, to the joy of their heart. Holy Spirit! guide, control, and make efficient. I seek not happiness or pleasure, — only to know and do God's will.

My soul is continually going up in earnest, agonizing prayer for the impenitent. Such intensity of feeling makes me quite sick.

The head, as well as the whole heart, is sick; but, with Moses and Paul, I could wish myself accursed that sinners might be saved. Still, O God! let me feel their worth. I cannot rest while souls are being eternally lost. Let me wear out, if I may; but let me know that some have found life by my death, and my rest will be sweet in heaven.

" Work, work, nor covet an ignoble rest:
 Allow no sloth thy spirit to beguile.

Those love the Saviour most who serve him
    best;
And he who blesses others shall be blest
With the full sunshine of his Saviour's smile."

GO, WORK TO-DAY IN MY VINEYARD.

Matt. xxi. 28.

Go, waiting one, and toil ;
The harvest-field is ready now and ripe :
Go gather in the sheaves from yonder soil,
    And come with new delight.

Go thou, and labor hard ;
Wield well the weapons on the field of life :
The foe is ever ready to retard
    When hottest is the strife.

Work thou with steady hand.
The Tempter's artful power is hard to foil;
His votaries are found in all the lands :
    Thou shouldst not cease to toil.

Work thou with earnest mind. `

How many wayward souls there are to win !

Oh ! bring them to the cross, where they may find

Forgiveness for their sin.

Stop not to heave a sigh ;

Rest not, though tired beneath the heavy load :

If thou wouldst reap, faint not 'midst deserts dry,

Or on the rugged road.

The crown that waits thee now

May far more bright and beautiful be made ;

And, when the angels place it on thy brow,

All toil will be repaid.

V.

PRAYER.

REQUENT, importunate, and protracted prayer is the link which closely unites the soul to Christ. I have decided, from this new year, to deprive myself of my morning nap, that I may have more time alone with God before entering upon the duties of the day.

Life is short: sometimes it seems all too short to attain to that perfect Christian character requisite to meet the King in his beauty.' " Evening and morning and at noon will I

pray, and cry aloud ; and He shall hear my
voice."

These are days of earnestness and weariness. Some days, I can pray without ceasing ;
while on others the wings of faith droop lan-
guidly, and the heavens seem brazen.

Last week was one of those interceding
weeks when every hour was burdened with
prayer for souls. My heart glows with ardent love for sinners. I will labor and pray :
duty done, the result, which is God's, must be
sure.

How I long to do something for this people !
but they are so difficult to reach. Oh that I
could raise them from their little narrow
world up to the glad light of Jesus' presence !
But I can pray. How great a privilege when
all other sources fail !

"I thank Thee, too, that thou hast made
　　Joy to abound ;
That, in the darkest spot of earth,
　　Some love is found :
I thank Thee more, that all our joy
　　Is touched with pain ;
That shadows fall on brightest hours;
　　That thorns remain ;
So that earth's bliss may be our guide,
　　And not our chain."

How sweet to commune with Jesus, — to
know the divine ear is bent to our petitions,
and our wants, pains, and griefs are all familiar to him ! " Casting all your care upon
him ; for he careth for you."

One week ago, dear M——, my soul in
prayer gained a new victory. For a long
time, I had been tempted severely. It seemed

that Satan would have me, that he might sift me as wheat. He tried to draw away my soul from its firm trust in God, and surround me with the darkness and mist of earth; but, praise God! he has not left my soul to Satan's power, but has sought me in my wanderings, and given me strong desires to turn unto him with all my soul.

Glory be to our God for salvation for ever and ever! All is upon the altar,—a living sacrifice accepted, unworthy as it is, through the blood of the Lamb.

My friends were unwilling that I should start on a journey of twelve hundred miles with my eyes in such an inflamed condition: but I had committed my way unto the Lord,—had prayed for his blessing upon the means used to restore them; and I felt the assurance that all would be well.

How blessed in life's perplexities, " By prayer and suplication, with thanksgiving, to make our requests known unto God "!

Hide me, O God! beneath the shadow of thy wing, till this calamity be overpast. Feel sick, nervous, and irritable. I go often and tell Jesus, and try to gather strength for the conflict.

Yes, " what time I am afraid, I will trust in Thee."

Mourn my languor in devotions. It is a great comfort, when I remember the " Spirit maketh intercessions with groanings that cannot be uttered." And Jesus, too, is praying for me.

How can I be languid? Rouse, my sluggish soul!

Arose early, and enjoyed a sweet hour with

God this morning. How refreshing the "bread from heaven"! All day I have been drinking from the fountain-head. Blessed Father! "all my springs are in thee."

Was enabled to draw so near to God in prayer, that I seemed wholly lost to self, and swallowed up in God. In my ardent desire for God, I cried out, "Crucify me, crucify me!" "Take all of earth from me, if needful; but give me an indwelling God!"

> "Come and possess me whole,
> And never hence remove!"

A little heart-ache to-night, but found Jesus quite ready to receive me when I went to tell him. Sweet Saviour! "A bruised reed shall he not break, and smoking flax shall he not quench."

Feel deeply my dependence upon God. My prayer is, "Thou alone canst help me;" and my song, "Other refuge have I none."

Eternity alone will reveal how many of the mercies I have received have been in answer to the petitions of kind, watchful Christian friends.

Have been waging warfare with the Enemy to-day; but, by the grace asked for in the morning, 1 came off conqueror, and at twilight enjoyed sweet, calm prayer and communion with the Triune God. "My grace shall be sufficient for thee." Oh strength for hands that hang down, and nerve for feeble knees!

Have been much troubled with wandering

thoughts : my mind was becoming weak and my soul barren, when I came importunately to the throne of grace, and held myself pleading for help, — present help to meet just this emergency.

Faith gained the victory ; and my thoughts were transferred from earth's worthless attractions to God, all and in all.

" When ye pray, believe that ye have the things ye ask for, and ye shall have them."

Such a sweet hour with God ! Gently the door of the senses swung together ; the world receded far away, and God filled all my thoughts.

Enjoyed the assurance that God was hearing prayer in behalf of C——. How sweet the privilege to unite with kindred minds at the mercy-seat ! Where two are agreed, what a mighty power they become in God !

We are so human, so selfish and wilful, that
we need much discipline. Holy Father! I
would have all the mind that was in Jesus.
Grant me patience in suffering, wisdom in
duty, humility in all my walk, and holiness
in all my conversation.

I thank God that we have One to guide us
who will lead us aright, if we closely follow
in the path of duty. Do you not feel stronger
each time your faith is thus tried? How
sweet it is, amid perplexity and doubt, to go
to our Father, and commit our way unto him,
seeking the guidance of the Holy Spirit! How
much safer we feel than with the instruction
of any earthly friend! for we know they are
but human and erring in their judgment; but
Jesus told us, when the Comforter came, he
should guide us into all truth.

I am often taught "how frail I am" when God refuses to answer my selfish prayers. He leads me to see wherein I have asked amiss.

Oh to see my vileness and ignorance in God's true light! then shall Christ be all.

I stood nearly alone in advocating the cause of the Master, and in trying to counteract the influences of sin and death.

On returning from the meeting to my room, I kneeled down ; but my heart was too full for utterance, and I simply looked a prayer, but all understood by the great Searcher of hearts. Long did I wait in communion with the Invisible, and arose in full possession of strength adequate to my need. Then was I able to say, " I can do all things through Christ strengthening me."

Have been obeying the divine injunction to-day, — "Pray without ceasing." The burden of my prayer has been for souls out of Christ.

Have been fasting with prayer; for "this kind goeth not out but by prayer and fasting." A condition of mind to wrestle effectually with God cometh by much self-denial.

The meeting this afternoon was glorious, and yet solemn on account of the presence of God. Have seldom witnessed so much of the glory and power of God. I hardly dared to raise my eyes to meet his awful presence.

Earnest prayers with tears were poured out. God cannot tarry. He will come to bless and save. "All things with God are possible." "Only believe."

Am enjoying very precious seasons of prayer. The Holy One draws near, and the whispers of his voice are music to the ear. The soul is bountifully fed in these seasons of communion. Oh, how we hunger for this spiritual bread! how soon our energies fail without it! "Lord, evermore give us this bread!"

The soul in steady and close communion with God is kept in perfect peace. Bless God!—in perfect peace amid the din and turmoil of earth.

Feel lonely and homesick; and yet no place seems so much like home as the bosom of Jesus. My hungry soul has never been satisfied from earthly sources but in drawing near to Christ.

Sweet Christ, I come! Let me approach even to the holy of holies through thy blood, and rest my weary heart on God!

The Spirit has called my attention to the fact, that before any important work, or

season of trial and temptation, the Saviour
spent long seasons in prayer and communion
with his Father. — Matt. iv. 2, 3; xiv. 23;
xxvi. 29.

Thus in our seasons of soul-hunger, and
when the heart is unusually drawn out in
prayer, God would have us seek supplies of
grace, which, in the hour of trial, we may use
for his glory, and our own growth and advance-
ment; for he anticipates our ills, and strength-
ens us for coming sorrow.

There is a heavy weight upon my heart.
To bear it, I am constantly reaching out for
God, and clinging to the Mighty One. Soothed
myself to sleep last night by repeating,
" God forsakes the righteous never; " and,
with morning's first consciousness, I was still
repeating, " Never! no, never! "

My hours of prayer are so precious! The spirit's ear catches the whispers of God, as he reveals to me the depths of his love and the grandeur of his power.

How happy the soul that holds converse with Deity! How insignificant do earthly joys seem when compared with an hour spent with God! Oh these quiet, happy hours! Can enjoy the society of Christians but little; but to be with God, and enjoy his presence, is all, — is heaven. Glory, glory!

During the past few days, the soul has been constantly stretching out arms of faith to grasp Christ. I have loved to sit by the window, and gaze up into the blue sky, where Christ sitteth at the right hand of the Father. It seems, when looking up, to bring the Triune God so near!

"My faith looks up to thee,
Thou Lamb of Calvary,
Saviour divine !
Now hear me while I pray ;
Take all my guilt away :
Oh, let me from this day
Be wholly thine ! "

I have need to pray without ceasing in these days of trial. My prayer is simply for grace, that I may endure and be patient.

If I bear up under the pressure, if I do not sink beneath my heavy weight of woe, I may bring much glory to God ; but, if I sink under my burden, God will be defeated in his holy purposes.

When I keep my eye fixed upon the suffering Christ, praying incessantly, then I feel strong ; but, if I dwell upon existing circumstances, I weep, and am so sad ! " When my spirit was overwhelmed within me, then Thou knewest my path."

Hope and trust alternate with doubting and sadness. Thoughts of my situation cause me to burst into tears ; but prayer quickly soothes the ruffled surface, and a smile takes the place of tears.

Oh the power of prayer ! How weary and dark would life be without it !

> " Help me, O Father ! when the world is pressing
> On my frail heart, which sinks without its friend :
> Help me, O Father ! let thy constant blessing
> Strengthen my weakness till the final end."

Have been having a tried, sad day, — a day in which we tire of things real and tangible, and seem to be held in constant communion with the spiritual and invisible. Have so many times ran to lay my head on Jesus' bosom, and tell him all !

I think, think of your great sorrow, till my heart grows sick with heavy thoughts. May Jesus bare his compassionate bosom, and take you in, while all his waves and billows are passing over you!

He trod the wine-press alone, and knows all your grief. Look unto him, and you shall find rest to your weary soul.

THE INVALID'S PRAYER.

Angel of patience, speed, speed thy flight;
Bring to my heart the rest that it needs;
Shed o'er my pillow soft beams of light;
Lead me by fountains and verdant meads:
Angel of patience, speed!
Soft as the zephyr through pending tresses,
Bow thy white wings through cloud-wildernesses;
Give to the spirit sweet dreaminesses, —
Dreams, sweet dreams, without pain!

Angel of patience, th e night is long;
 Starlight and moonbeams bring me not sleep:
Shade thou the stars the bright worlds among;
 Bid the lone moonbeams lie still and weep:
  Angel of patience, shade!
Music in wildest strains, pensive and deep,
Comes from the forest-pine where fairies keep,
Bringing back memories painfully sweet:
  Angel of patience, weep!

Loved ones are passing before me to-night,
 Phantom-like, flitting throughout the scene:
Spread out thy pinions, and hide the light,
 Filling the past with its gold and sheen, —
  Beautiful gold and sheen!
Stay thou to calm the wild fever-flow now;
Loosen this band of dull pain from my brow;
Lovingly, tenderly, over me bow:
  Angel of patience, stay!

Angel of patience, I feel thy power:
 Purer submission thou'st brought to me;

Turned my sad thoughts to a better hour.

When the tired spirit released shall be

From weariness and pain,

Then in God's paradise, fresh and vernal,

Where is the city with gates eternal,

I shall drink ever of joys supernal, —

Drink from the chalice of God.

VI.

PATIENCE.

HOW the discipline of life changes all the fanciful visions of youth! How it prunes the offshoots of imagination, and crumbles the castles it was such a delight to build! Bless God for discipline constant and severe! It opens the eyes, and shows us what life is; it removes the curtain that hides the only place of surety and rest, and shows us the home of the blest so plainly, that the hour of departure cannot be dreaded.

No two years have the same discipline ; but, as we advance toward God, the conflict seems to increase in strength and power.

> " When, through deepest seas of sorrow,
> We have gained the heavenly shore,
> Bliss from every wave we'll borrow,
> And for each will love Thee more."

Sometimes my feet grow weary with this long, rough path of suffering; but I plod on, leaning heavily upon the promises, — "Yet will not I forget thee. Thy name is graven upon the palms of my hands: thy walls are continually before me."

The Fair opened to-day. I have thought of the tastefully-arranged hall, the motley crowds, the happy greetings, the music and speeches ; and sometimes I have seemed almost there myself: but the iron grasp of intense pain would quickly bring me back again.

I have tried to suffer patiently, happily, knowing that it was the divine appointment, and that others could do no more than act their appointed part well.

My poor nerves have become so jaded with the suffering of the past week, that I seem to regard nothing in its true light but Jesus. He seems the same lovely Being, the same tried Friend. Am sad and depressed, yet not unhappy. Suppose it is simply a nervous depression. "He knoweth our frame : he remembereth that we are dust."

"Who are these arrayed in white robes ? and whence came they ? These are they which came up out of great tribulation, and washed their robes, and made them white in the blood of the Lamb."

While suffering intensely last evening, the question arose in my mind, "Am I washing my robes by bearing this patiently?" The thought made me strong.

> "Oh! fear not in a world like this,
>   And thou shalt know ere long, —
> Know how sublime a thing it is.
>   To suffer and be strong.
>
> Yes, in a trial-world like this,
>   Where all that comes is sent,
> Learn how divine a thing it is
>   To smile and be content."

These are precious lines, my sister. God grant that we may know what it is to leave all to our Father's will! Though clouds may hover around us, we will look up, as we hear him whisper, "Fear not, little flock," and "smile and be content."

Those lone, sad heart-wailings are ever

echoing through the inner depths of my sympathetic soul. I long to lay your throbbing head and heart upon my own, where, aided by sympathy's power, you can weep calmly, yet profusely, as falls the summer rain.

I know you appear calm ; but to do so, with the wild tumult of the soul, you strain every nerve to its highest point of tension, till it can vibrate no more. Dear M——, I cannot feel the dreadful weight of woe that presses upon your soul ; I know not the blackness of darkness that surrounds it ; I feel not those chill, wintry winds that ice your very being (winter is when those we love have perished ; for the heart ices then): but I do know that one of the greatest sorrows that falls to the lot of woman has burst in all its fearfulness and gloom upon your desolate life.

Your noble, devoted husband has fallen. He was the shrine upon which you laid all of earthly love, desire, or hope: that taken, your gems are scattered, shattered, and shrineless for earthly hours; but in the soul there rises up a heavenly temple, upon the walls of which is inscribed, "Thy will, O God! be done."

These are words wrung from the agony of a Saviour's heart; and while you so patiently drink your bitter, bitter cup, he weeps, and loves you still.

"Beside the toilsome way
    An angel softly walks,
With pale, sweet face, and eyes cast meekly down,
The while, from withered leaves and flowerless
      stalks,
    She weaves my fitting crown.

'Patience!' she sweetly saith:
'The Father's mercies never come too late.
Gird thee with patient strength and trusting faith,
    And firm endurance: wait!'"

It will all be well in our Father's time. I only need much patience.

The billows of grief are rolling and foaming, and tossing against my heart. Like long-pent waters, they are rushing over my soul in all their madness ; and I live only by thinking, " God is not dead." Jesus lives; Jesus lives forever ! I will try to

" Think of the gain only, count not the losses ;
   Think of the crown only, not of the crosses ;
   Think of the angels surrounding the throne ;
   Think of the victory, the song, and the crown."

Fast Day. — Feel like running down the vista of the past ; but it makes me too sad. I must trust, and be happy. The year has been one of suffering, but one during which I have felt the power of religion as never before.

Ample grace, that makes affliction welcome !

The thought occurs to me, as the moments pass by, "And what am *I* doing?" Faith answers, "Lying still, and letting God's will be done as it is done by the angels in heaven." This passive life yields an experience rarely known to them to whom life's active part is given. It is born of suffering, nourished in struggle and victory, and matures in silent glory.

I have tried (and it has not been hard with so much help from God) to bear all my sufferings uncomplainingly, and to kiss the rod that deals each blow. It seems great condescension in my heavenly Father to so love me as to choose just that path for me that will most conduce to my spiritual growth. Blessed Father, I love thy chastening; and "though thou slay me, yet will I trust in thee."

I am trying to be resigned. God offers no cup to our lips that he will not enable us to drink. How precious is the inspired word ! — " Fear thou not, for I am with thee ; be not dismayed, for I am thy God. I will strengthen thee ; I will help thee ; yea, I will uphold thee with the right hand of my righteousness."

> " God and Father! thou didst give me
> Sorrow for my portion here ;
> But thy mercy will not leave me
> Helpless, struggling with despair.
> For to thee, when sad and lonely,
> Unto thee alone, I turn,
> And to thee, my Father, only,
> Look for comfort when I mourn ;
> And my spirit waxes stronger,
> And my trembling heart is still,
> And my bosom doubts no longer
> Thine inexorable will."

I breathe from out my inmost heart, " Thy

will be done!" It is but a little while that
we shall know the bitterness of deprivation;
and then all the privileges of heaven will
be ours, and that forever.

How holy would I walk here, that I may be
near God there! I would be like Christ now,
that, when the glad trump shall sound, I may
awake in his likeness.

My head at times is so tight and numb! and
then the tightness seems to break into a thou-
sand shivers of pain, all through the brain!
To think or pray seems like raising a heavy
weight upon the brain. This is only one
pain; but the sum total cannot equal your
heart-pain. How great a sorrow has fallen
upon your life! Only God knows of its depth;
only God's pity can reach your great life-
need. All of his heart of tenderness is yours
and mine. Thank God, all of infinite love
and sympathy is ours!

I cannot help clinging to the thought, that
after God has thoroughly "purged" these
tabernacles of defilement, that after he has
fully fitted us for what he has in store for us
here or hereafter, he will, even here, give
us a little season of prosperity, and a little rest
from life's heaviest crosses. But, be it as it
may, "let the Lord do as seemeth him
good." Yes, the heart responds from its
very depths, "Amen and amen!"

"And welcome, precious, can His Spirit make
    My little drop of suffering for his sake.
Father, the cup I drink, the path I take,
        All, all, is known to thee."

How sweet the thought that He does know
all, and can sympathize with us in every sorrow and pain!

Praise God! Thou knowest all our path.

We will keep close to thee, follow thy footsteps, that we may not be lost in the intricate
windings of earth.

How much we have to make us happy,
though the angel of sorrow ever walks by our
side! If one love dies by the way, we have
others left to love, and for whom we should
love to live, that we may make their lives
happy. The closet is ever a place of sunshine,
where we may catch gleams of all that is
bright and beautiful.

Let us not forget how much we have left,
though something is constantly being taken.

"All is yours, and ye are Christ's, and
Christ is God's."

Oh this longing, longing, restless heart!
And yet, as I asked myself the question,
"Where and what should I like to be, could I

choose for myself?" I was cheerfully able to reply, "Just what I am and where I am; for the place of my Father's choosing must be the best." Yes: be still, thou ever-restless heart, and know thy God doeth all things well.

"As many as I love, I rebuke and chasten." Sweet, sweet thought! "As many as I love." How true, when God has purposes of his own, he allows people to love or dislike us! The universal love and interest I have had shown me by a certain class I have ever considered was the gift of God: so now do I recognize the divine will in the non-interest and coldness of those around me. Oh the divine will! How sweet to repose upon it amid the tossings of life! How sweet the divine love when human love fails!

Thanksgiving. — With morning's first con-

sciousness, I tried to thank God for my pains.
If I could do any good; if I could show to
those around me the power of religion, and
how sweetly the grace of God supports and
sustains the soul, — how willing, even happy,
should I be to endure any amount of pain! I
would love to do something for God. The
love of self wanes; and my love for God
burns brighter every day. I could do or bear
any thing for him.

God is perfecting you through suffering.
Oh! if you can be perfect, shrink not, though
the furnace be heated " seven times hotter "
than is wont; for the presence of the Fourth
will surely be with you.

May you continually feel that " your heavenly Father knoweth that ye have need of all
these things "! Our Father often allows us to
suffer while engaged in promoting his cause.

So did Jesus suffer in his earth-work; and we may not expect to be above our Master and Lord.

Almost a sleepless night; but I love to suffer. I love the gift of God, — my pains. Wish I were very much more patient. Miss R—— said the other day, " You are willing to bear every thing." But I questioned, " Does God think so ? " It is what God thinks of us, and not man merely.

I am conscious of being more humble and patient. Affliction does make us more like the " Man of sorrows." If not now, we shall know hereafter why God has thus led us " about." God afflicts for our profit and his glory. While we are strengthened by overcoming the obstructions in the way, God is glorified in the development and use of that strength.

Strangely checkered are the scenes of life. How blessed to have one immutable source to which we can flee! My heart has been filled with grief, my cup pressed down with sorrow: but I have tried very hard to be patient; to hold still, and behold God's workings. God overrules the minutiæ of life, as well as the powers of the earth.

Nothing can befall us but what is best. I will not murmur or complain, but, with trusting heart, will " be still."

> " Smoothly along we cannot sail :
> One day the calm, one day the gale ;
> Ever the rocks on either side,
> Ever the prow against the tide."

I am busy all the time, doing little fancy jobs for my friends, as I go about among them ; but it does not seem much. It is not my idea of life to crochet, embroider, &c. But this thought constantly cheers me: "Whatever God appoints becomes a high and holy duty, worth doing well and bravely."

It is the patient continuance in well-doing that is the great test. It is very easy doing a great work that is soon accomplished, when we can throw all of our energies and heart into it; but the daily performance of homely duties requires a strong love to the Father's will. Yet here I am, my Father! "Sacrifice and offering thou didst not desire, else would I have given it thee. Lo, O God! I delight to do thy will."

"O land of rest! for thee I sigh,"

sings the worn spirit; but when I see so many unprepared for that rest, with faith in Him who has promised strength, I bow in humble submission, doing cheerfully the duties

assigned me, while I sing a yet sweeter song,
— "Thy will be done."

One has beautifully said, " There are morn-
ings of life which never have an evening."
Then we will toil on in the way our Father
has marked out; and if he calls us in the
morning, noon, or evening of life, God grant
that our work may be done, and well done!
For days, my heart has felt the force of Mil-
ton's words : —

> " God does not need man's work or his own gifts.
> Who best bear his mild yoke, they serve him best;
> Who best can suffer, best can do ; best reign,
> Who first well hath obeyed."

Perfect obedience! Faith scans it; but I
cannot reach it at one bound. It must be a
life-work.

I am safe in the hands of Jesus in life or in

death. I dare not trust myself to choose; but I can trust all to Him " who is too wise to err, too good to be unkind." All my desire, O God! is that thy will should be done, and thy name glorified. Give or take, smite or heal, sweet or bitter be my portion, yet, O Father! glorify thyself in me.

My path has been rugged: but, if it leads me home, the roughness of the journey will all be forgot ; or, if remembered, it will only add a sweeter strain to my song, and make heaven dearer.

> "From darkness here, and dreariness,
>   We ask not full repose :
>   Only be Thou at hand to bless
>   Our trial-hour of woes.
>   Is not the pilgrim's toils o'erpaid
>   By the clear rill and palmy shade ?
>   And see we not up earth's dark glade
>   The gate of heaven unclose ? "

I love to press my bared feet into every foot-
print of the Saviour's; for I find every thorn
hallowed by his blood and sufferings. Sweet
privilege, to have any experience similar to
his own!

"Unto you it is given in the behalf of
Christ, not only to believe on his name, but
also to suffer for his sake."

O disease, thou ruthless destroyer of our
bright hopes! couldst thou not have tarried
a few short years, till we had labored a little
for our God? Then we might have returned
from our field of labor " with rejoicing, bearing our sheaves with us," and, fitted for the
bowers of Paradise when God should call,
enter in with those whom he had given us, to
go no more out forever. Ah, no! thou camest
at the bidding of our kind Father; and we
will welcome thee now, knowing thy mission

is one of love and mercy. "Surely it were never His design who placed us here that we should live in ease, or drink at Pleasure's fountain."

Dear G——, do you ever sincerely thank God that you are not poor, and that you have kind friends to supply your needs? When money and health too are gone, life has many a hard struggle, many an up-hill path.

I would not have this allusion savor of discontent. No, no! I thank God for my poverty and my pains. He gives me sweet and tender tokens of his love, which counterbalance all of earthly good withheld.

I was only thinking, if earth's favored children could but realize their blessings, and possess the heavenly heritage too, their cup must be running over with joy; for, with the little of earth that has fallen to my lot, I am

very,very happy; because God is all and in
all

One day nearer home! How it cheers my
weary heart! The trials of this day are all
passed through, never to be experienced
again, and now can be subtracted from the
sum total. Praise God, praise God! Each
day's strength is apportioned, while we work
out our salvation with fear and trembling.

Sometimes I feel I can endure this nervous
wear no longer : then comes the thought, —

> " One by one thy trials wait thee ;
> Do not fear an armèd band :
> Some will fade as others greet thee, —
> Shadows passing through the land."

When I feel my limbs so numb, hanging like weights to the body, my very. being
quivers with fear; but I try not to dwell

upon the dim uncertainties of the future
gloomily. Hope lends Fancy her bright wings,
and I see myself walking about again, erect,
sprightly, as I am wont to do, taking some
part in the active duties of life, and doing
something for God and the world. But, in
health or pain, God's will shall be my delight.

How faithful are the promises of our blessed
Saviour! How near he has been to you, ever
whispering, " Lo, I am with you alway"!
" Bear these sufferings for me a little longer;
and, instead of the ' crown of thorns ' which
is now piercing your patient brow, I will give
a crown of never-fading glory." A little
while, and the long age of bliss in heaven is
yours. " In my Father's house are many mansions : if it were not so, I would have told you."

Many shadows have flitted across my horizon to-day. Why this restless feeling, this chafing against the iron bars of circumstance?

Does not God do all things well? "Doth he not see my ways, and count all my steps?"

I cannot doubt it, and will cheerfully acquiesce in all that he apportions me.

With a steady faith, the shadows cannot linger long; for, when Jesus sees the upturned faces of his little ones, he is "touched" with the feelings of their infirmity, and quickly bids the darkness flee, while he, with healing in his wings, rises in the heart, the glad Sun of Righteousness.

THE SUFFERER'S SOLILOQUY.

I'm very tired and worn!
So many years of torturing pain
Have come and gone, and come again:
The night brings ne'er a morn.

The end I cannot see:
The wormwood draught, the bitter cup,
As to my lips I take it up,
    Seems deep and full to me.

In life's fair morn how bright
My hopes, teeming with freshest life!
I did not dream that earth was rife
    With shadows, it seemed so light.

On high my life-sun stood
In its meridian power;
My heart exultant every hour
    In some new earthly good.

Ah me! then came the storm,
Surging my life in deep distress,
Steeping my soul in bitterness,
    Leaving me sad, forlorn.

Yet was it not the love
And tenderness of God to me,

13

That did appoint the cross? Ay: we
Cannot see as they above.

The suffering and loss,
The darkness shrouding all in gloom,
Have made me seek the heavenly home,
And cling to Christ's dear cross.

Yes, I'm very tired and worn!
" But weakest ones have largest share
Of the Shepherd's tender care; "
And in his arms I'm borne.

A little while to stay,
And then our sufferings will be done:
Be strong, my soul! with patience run
All the appointed way.

VII.

WAITING.

OW sweet to rest on His will who doeth all things well, not only when he commands us to go forward, but also when he bids us pause and wait! "His purposes are ripening fast, unfolding every hour;" and, in the best way possible, he is fitting us for our earthly mission. Though human sight may not discern it in the many interruptions of our chosen plans, yet faith whispers, "All things shall work together for good to them that love God."

.

While I wait, I dare not take my thoughts from Christ, lest I doubt. To thee, O Christ! I cling. Immutable Christ! to thee I cling. "Wait on the Lord; be of good courage; and he shall strengthen thine heart: wait, I say, on the Lord." Is not this a command parallel with "Speak unto the children of Israel, that they go forward"? Does not the one, as well as the other, require cheerful obedience? I will lay hold upon the promise, —"He shall strengthen thine heart;" then can I happily "wait," and "be of good courage."

For several days, the shadows have come between my soul and Christ. I think I may have been too anxious to do some great work

for God, and have overlooked the little ways
of usefulness. It has been a hard lesson for
me, that God did not need my services. I
know that he needs none of us; but he does
design to use some of us: and it is not easy to
be satisfied, when day after day passes, and no
work is given me to do for Jesus. Truly,
there are many such days when all my work
is waiting.

> " One sweetly solemn thought
> Comes to me o'er and o'er, —
> I'm nearer home to-day
> Than I've ever been before ;
> Nearer my Father's house,
> Where the many mansions be ;
> Nearer the great white throne ;
> Nearer the crystal sea ;
> Nearer that bound of life
> Where we lay our burdens down ;
> Nearer leaving our cross ;
> Nearer wearing our crown."

Sweet, sweet thought! I repeat it again and again, and each time it seems a more blessed reality. Glory to God! "nearer home!" It fills my soul with joy. Cares, pains, trials, come, if ye will: each day brings me nearer the end. Soon I shall be free, and dwell with Christ at home. No more fatigue, no more distress, but joy and happiness forever. Shall we not raise one loud shout of "Home at last, home at last!"

I used to feel almost unhappy when I could not labor; but now I am learning to be quite happy in waiting. God is giving me a more cheerful and perfect submission. How far it has been from being perfect in character! Thank God that he leads us on step by step, teaching us some new lesson every day!

Down by the river : —

> "How can you call me back to earth
> When I am almost home ?
> How can I turn away from those
> Who beckon me to come ?
>
> How can I leave the starry crown
> Which I in heaven may wear,
> And hold this weary, weary cross,
> Which is so hard to bear ? "

These many months I have been waiting to know my Father's will. I hear no voice bidding me to do this or that. I know not where the next step may lead ; but I press on, as light falls upon my way. Jesus whispers, " What I do thou knowest not now ; but thou shalt know hereafter." I have committed all to the Lord. Doing or suffering, I am his. " It is good that a man should both hope and quietly wait for the salvation of the Lord."

"Nearer the port by every wave!"

Praise God! Even now I see my Father's house, peering in the distance. A few more struggles, and the conflict will be ended. We shall have fought the fight, and finished our course; and blessed will it be if we can say with the servant of God, "I am now ready to be offered."

Sometimes when the love of God burns brightly upon the altar of my heart, when I think of so much to be done, when I think of souls rushing unsaved into eternity, I find it difficult to rest, and hush the throbbings of my eager spirit. But I am making it a point of duty; and, since I offered myself a "living sacrifice," all duty is pleasant, even that of a passive character, so uncongenial to our active natures.

The heart is calmly stayed upon God. The whisper came in prayer, " Be still, and know that I am God." By this continued waiting, God is teaching me lessons of faith. Yes, my heart, " be still : " God knows why.

" Behold, we live through all things, — famine, thirst,
Bereavement, pain, all grief and misery,
All woe and sorrow. Life inflicts its worst
On soul and body ; but we cannot die.
Though we be sick and tired and faint and worn,
Lo ! all things can be borne."

Ah ! the day is fast approaching, when, upon the banks of the celestial river, we shall repeat the story of our earth-wanderings, and rejoice in Him who hath redeemed us, and brought us thither. Glory to Jesus for the beautiful prospect! My heart beats high for heaven, but is none the less strong for the conflict and the completion of my earth-mission.

Cloud and sunshine in nature, and in my own heart too.

> " Some rain into all lives must fall ;
>   Some days must be dark and dreary."

I wait, looking unto Jesus for the blessed evening-time of light.

> " Angel! behold, I wait,
>   Wearing the thorny crown through all life's hours ;
> Wait, till thy hand shall ope the eternal gate,
>   And change the thorns to flowers."

WAITING.

" All the days of my appointed time will I wait till my change comes."

Waiting, waiting, calmly waiting,
As the days pass slowly by;

Sitting near the cross of Jesus;
Waiting till the shadows fly.

Waiting, waiting, till the sunlight
Gilds the eastern way of faith;
Waiting for the voice of Jesus,
As the holy prophet saith.

Waiting, waiting, yet am serving :
That is all that is required ;
Suffering the will of Jesus,
While the heart with love is fired.

How this ardent wish to labor
Burns the censer of the soul,
While we're foiled in each endeavor,
Vainly struggling for the goal!

We are living stones, and precious :
Well the workman does his part, —
Burnishing the rougher edges,
Making perfect these poor hearts.

Waiting, waiting! Holy Father!
　Thou the vessel wilt prepare,
Fitting it for thine own glory,
　Making it thy tender care.

And if this is all my mission,
　Here to suffer and to wait,
Let the heart, in meek submission,
　Still rejoice at such a fate.

VIII.

LONGINGS.

ND I shall be happy in heaven! How much, sometimes, I long to be there! My poor life seems so broken and unsatisfactory, that I want to be where Jesus is, and be satisfied. "I shall be satisfied!" Wonderful words! but not till we awake in His likeness shall we fully comprehend.

Feel more tenderness of heart than usual. I am hungering for more grace, more love, to

dwell more fully in Jesus. The blood of
Christ is my only plea. How precious the
thought, " it cleanseth " !

I would hasten on to the kingdom. Oh this
loitering ! how it chills the ardor of our. love,
and presses the soul with a heavy weight !
Help, Father, when we pray !

My poor heart trembles often ; but I hold
fast, and cling to the Mighty One. " A little
while," — what sweet words to us here ! but
there will be no " little while " in heaven, but
endless joy. How blessed it will be to be
there, to be with Jesus, and see him as he is !

> " My God, my Life, my Sanctified,
> My Saviour, and my All ! "

That is heaven.

Jerusalem, the city of God, our city, our

home, precious and sweet; and so near us !
Only a step, and we reach it. "They hunger
no more, neither thirst any more." What
a soul-inspiring thought! We shall have so
much of Jesus, that we shall feel no more
hungerings and thirstings after him, but have
a continual feast. We shall never feel a want
of him, because we shall ever sit at his table.
Some think these words of holy John refer
alone to the wants of the body. But why need
we think only of bodily cravings? Are not
our souls ever hungry in this earthly taber-
nacle? Is not the sweetness of the promise
realized when we regard it only in a spiritual
sense? Herein can I trace spiritual growth
in my soul, — that the words of Jesus find a
place in the depths of the heart, and give life
to the spirit.

Beyond the blooming and the fading,

I shall be soon ;

Beyond the shining and the shading,

Beyond the hoping and the dreading,

I shall be soon.

Love, rest, and home,

Sweet home !

Lord, tarry not, but come.

Oh for a heart fired with the love of Jesus and his cause! Oh for a love that will embrace weary, dying souls, and bring them to the cross !

An earnest looking to Jesus, a thirsting for living waters. I must have much of God, or I cannot be a power sufficient to move sinners about me. Strange, when these fallen natures are renewed, and we are made in the sweet image of Jesus, how the wicked fall before us !

Heaven is becoming daily more attractive. Will it not be sweet to lay off this dull mortality, and be able to commune with each other by thought, with more than electric rapidity, however widely separated in space? We shall be present to each other in thought, though the field of our exploration be in space infinitely distant. Blessed hope! cheering prospect!

I will not grow weary in well-doing; for the crown of the faithful is awaiting me now.

Oh to sit down with Jesus, and drink the new wine in our Father's kingdom! The time is short. Soon at home. But, while the Master tarries, let me " watch and be sober," redeeming the time, because the days are evil. Would have my soul so filled with Christ, that every thought may be pure and holy.

"No foot of land do I possess, —
A stranger in this wilderness ; "

but, " in my Father's house, there are many mansions." I shall soon know the extent of my legacy, and enter into its fulness forever. While I tarry, an abiding peace makes my heart glad.

These day-dreams seem more sad than the reality. They do not encourage the sunshine, but leave the heart shadowy, damp, and chilly. But this dreamy state of mind seems quite essential to some spirits. It is the way that leads to that high region of thought and ex-perience, where we wake from our dreams to the sweet reality of things immortal ; where we no longer pass the time in building castles in the air, but base our lives firmly and posi-tively upon the will of God.

Ah, me! do you not love to think of that narrow little bed where we shall stretch the tired limbs, and rest, rest, rest? "Though worms destroy this body, yet in my flesh shall I see God." "There the wicked cease from troubling, and there the weary be at rest."

"As the hart panteth for the water-brooks, so panteth my soul for thee, O God! When shall I come, and appear before God?" This is the language of my heart. Nothing do I desire so much as God. He alone satisfies my fainting spirit.

My heart aches, aches, aches! I grow old and tired. My desires for others, and their carelessness, make earth a sad place to me. I long for heaven, —

"Love, rest, and home :
Lord, tarry not, but come."

I shall not be as busy by and by, and hope to take some rest. Rest? Nay, not till I get home. When I think of Jesus, I want to go home ; but, when I see so much to be done, I cry out, " Send me ! " I love to tell of God's love and bounty, his marvellous stores, — and all ours !

How glad I am there is an eternity ! We shall need it all to sound His praise.

While busy with my hands to-day, I have been singing, —

> " Nearer, my God, to thee, —
> Nearer to thee."

My soul has been reaching out for God.

> " E'en though it be a cross that raiseth me,"

yet would I be drawn near to thee, my God !

How easily I become interested in earthly

things! Oh that I could ever keep so near to
Jesus as to be dazzled with his beauty and
loveliness!

I do love him above every thing ; but I want
my love more deep, constant, and ardent.

" Heaven is not reached at a single bound ;
    But we build the ladder by which we rise
    From the lowly earth to the vaulted skies,
And we mount to its summit round by round.

I count this thing to be grandly true, —
    That a noble deed is a step toward God,
    Lifting the soul from the common sod
To a purer air and a broader view.

We hope, we resolve, we aspire, we pray ;
    And we think we mount the air on wings,
    Beyond the recall of sensual things,
While our feet still cling to the heavy clay.

Wings for the angels, but feet for the men !
We may borrow the wings to find the way ;
We may hope and resolve, and aspire and
pray :
But our feet must rise, or we fall again. ”

To be a partaker of Christ's holiness, — to
be clothed with his rightcousness, — must it
not be a˙blessed lot ? How much I crave a
deeper experience of such bliss !

If we are united to him, all is well. No
matter what may be the portion allotted to us,
if Christ and his strength are ours, we need
ask no more.

A heavy rain fell last night, and the earth
is looking so fresh and beautiful this morning!
My thirsty soul is panting for a fresh shower
of divine grace. Come, Jesus! oh, come to
me now, and water thine own habitation from
the living springs!

Stormy and dark without, and the sunshine of God's smiles gleams but dimly through the mists of earth. Sweet land of sunshine and beauty eternal, I long for thee !

Oh for a deeper entrance into the heart of God's love! Would not that silence our murmurings, and lead us to repose with confidence upon Infinite Wisdom ?

DAY–DREAMS.

I am dreaming by the window,
  As the shades of evening fall, —
Dreaming sad and shady day-dreams,
  Such as sometimes come to all.

I am dreaming by the window
  Of the by-gone fraught with tears :
E'en my childhood sorrowful, and
  Sadder still these later years.

I am dreaming by the window ;
Dreaming of the household band;
Dreaming of the broken circle
Severed by the Father's hand.

I am dreaming by the window.
Spirit-forms, methinks, I see :
Spectral in the evening twilight,
They have come once more to me.

I am dreaming by the window,
Looking out into the night.
One by one, the stars smile on me :
Something whispers, " God does right."

God does right : he took my loved ones,
Let my earthly idols fall.
God does right the shades to lengthen ;
God does right : he's all in all !

I am dreaming by the window ;
Dreaming of the other shore ;
Dreaming of the tears all banished
When we wake to dream no more.

www.ingramcontent.com/pod-product-compliance
Lightning Source LLC
Chambersburg PA
CBHW030129030726

47498CB00007B/2624